THE COSTUME OF THE THEATRE

LOUIS XIV AS LE ROI SOLEIL

Habit français à la Romaine

Bibliothèque Nationale, Paris

THE
COSTUME OF THE
THEATRE

By
THEODORE KOMISARJEVSKY

NEW YORK
HENRY HOLT AND COMPANY

Authorized Edition

Printed 1932

PRINTED IN THE
UNITED STATES OF AMERICA

TO

THE MEMORY

OF MY FATHER

T. P. KOMISARJEVSKY

INTRODUCTION

TOTUS mundus agit histrionem—or, everyone in this world of ours struts it like an actor. Men and women, especially the latter, shew their histrionic longings and abilities to a large degree in the way in which they dress themselves in real life, and in their unrestrained interest in what is known as "la mode." For many centuries now, the latter has been created for them by fashion designers, who cunningly exploit the people's weakness for "play-acting" in real life, and who themselves play the producer's rôle in these spectacular life-pageants, treating the inhabitants of our world as so many supers in their pageants.

The stage costumes, merely accentuating those fashions worn in life, or interpreting period dresses in the modern spirit, express the theatrical attitude of the world with even more intensity than the everyday life costumes themselves.

The costume of the theatre has always seemed to me a fascinating subject, even when regarded from the amateur view-point, and not from that of the theatrical professional; I therefore hope that this book will not only prove useful to those who work on the stage, but will also interest and entertain those who have no connection with the theatre.

I have not attempted to write a "complete history" of costume in the theatre, for, indeed, in one volume this would be an impossible undertaking. I offer these pages merely as an essay upon the subject, its origins, the stage at different periods in theatrical history, together with the various countries and people who influenced Theatrical Costume.

I would like to remember here with gratitude the sympathy of Hélène, Felix, Fritz, and Misha Koessler; also of Elfriede Jarosy, in whose hospitable house on the quiet lake of Gründlsee I thought out this book and wrote some of its chapters.

October 1931.   T. K.

vii

CONTENTS

ILLUSTRATIONS

CHAPTER I

COSTUME AND THE MAN

TO look beautiful. To assume importance. To appeal sexually. These are the human aspirations upon which Dame Fashion has invariably worked when creating what is called *costume*.

From any practical and rational viewpoint costume would seem to be a useless and even "silly" invention, its origins being of an æsthetic, ostentatious, and "immoral" nature. These have nothing in common with the origins of *clothing,* which are rooted in essentially utilitarian or moral motives.

The essential concern of clothing is to cover up the human body and protect it from the vagaries of climate and the hardships of labour, regardless of any feeling for the beauty of the forms, proportions, or the colouring of the body. Apart from the necessity caused by climatic, working, and economic conditions, clothing has also evolved from various moral and religious doctrines, which have instilled a sense of physical shame into people. These doctrines, advocating modesty, demanded that the body, and especially the sexually attractive parts of it, should be hidden by garments.

In Italy still at the present time women are forbidden to enter Roman Catholic churches in sleeveless and low-necked dresses even during the hottest weather, and no female can be admitted into the presence of the Pope unless she is bandaged from her toes to her chin, and wears a veil to hide her seductive hair and to throw a shadow on her sinful face.

The difficult problem of defining modesty and its opposite in feminine fashions was solved about a year ago by the International Congress of Women's Catholic Leagues in Rome. A long and

1

animated discussion took place as to the best way of putting into practice the principles enunciated by the Church. A resolution was then passed in conformity with the Italian delegates' proposal that modest attire must fulfil the following conditions:

Dresses must extend from the neck to below the calf.

Sleeves must fall below the elbow.

Clothes must not adhere to the body or be transparent.

Stockings must not be either transparent or flesh-coloured.

As a result of such a resolution a manager of a Milan theatre was fined for permitting girls belonging to an Austrian revue on tour in Italy "to appear on the stage without tights and dressed in a manner contrary to morality."

In Egypt a Bill has been submitted quite recently to Parliament to prevent women from appearing in public in short sleeves or low-necked dresses, which are described as immoral. The Bill stipulates that women who appear in the streets in such attire shall be twice warned by a husband or guardian. For a third offence the penalty is a £20 fine or seven days' imprisonment.

Costume has evolved from a desire on the part of men and women to beautify themselves, pandering to vanity and to the æsthetic and sexual sense, and from that "theatrical" spirit strong in most people, which creates a desire to escape from prosaic reality and to appear as something "other."

Often resorting to cunning artificialities, costume decorates the human figure to show it to what is considered the best advantage and to increase the sexual appeal of the wearer. It takes into consideration the architecture of the human body, seeking to accentuate and to improve its forms. It heightens the general effect of the human figure by harmonizing the colouring of the adornments with the tones of the flesh, eyes, and hair of the wearer. The shape of the costume is dictated either by the ensemble of all the forms of the body (as in the costume of the primitives and the Antiques) or by certain forms of the figure only (as in the European costume of the Christian era). As the main purpose of costume is to decorate the body, the naked flesh always enters as an inevitable part in the composition of the costume. As the natural naked body is seldom æsthetically attractive, the decorations of the body are aiming at correcting and hiding its defects. A really beautiful body is even spoiled by too much decoration. The fashionable French portrait painter, Jean-Gabriel Domergue, says that "les hommes ou les femmes qui sont beaux nus sont mal une fois habillés." As beauty can rarely subordinate itself to climatic or economic conditions, so costume often demands that the wearer shall sacrifice bodily comfort and a large proportion of his, and more especially of her, financial resources. Referring to the question of discomfort of costume, the French sum it up in the saying: "Pour être beau il faut souffrir," and everyone knows how many poor husbands have been drawn into the bankruptcy courts on account of their wives' love of dress.

The widespread belief that the costume reveals the man and is an index to his character is quite wrong. For a good many centuries past costume has merely revealed certain outlooks and tendencies of the epoch which have created the particular form, but have levelled the appearance of individuals. It is the spirit and taste of a small group of originators of fashion and their cunning knowledge of the psychology of people which are revealed in the creation of what is called "la mode." It is the herd instinct in humanity which prompts them to behave in a manner forced upon them by stronger wills and imaginations, and in the matter of costume, snobbishness and the desire to emulate one's "betters" have been largly responsible for the establishment of fashions. "We may eat according to our own appetite, but in our apparel must follow the fashion of the multitude with whom we live" (Fynes Moryson, *Itinerary*, 1617). It is only in the details of the costume and the way in which it is worn that the individuality of the wearer can be revealed.

The Southern primitives, who, because of their climatic conditions, did not need protective clothing, may be considered as the originators of costume. These people were believers in a more significant world beyond the immediate actuality, the realm of their grotesque fantastic gods. They strove through imagination to fathom the mysteries of that world, and tried to resemble the appearance of the gods which they had created themselves as expressions of that beyond. For this theatrical purpose and without any other practical reason they decorated their nakedness, which for them was a natural state, and of which they were not ashamed, and saw no reason to conceal. Modesty was unknown to the primitives by nature, because originally the sense of shame was only associated with the "psyche" and not with the physique.

What useful or moral purpose could there be in a naked savage wearing bits of fur on his back under the hottest sun, or in having a ring clamped to his nostrils, or in tattooing, or in a piece of ivory or in a disc stuck through his lip? The story of a black chieftain who received the gift of some garments from a European and, instead of covering his naked body with them, tore them into small pieces, which he distributed to his suite to be worn as ornaments, is typical.

Stendhal wrote that "les trois quarts de la pudeur sont une chose apprise. Une femme de Madagascar laisse voir sans y songer ce qu'on cache le plus ici, mais mourrait de honte plutôt que de montrer son bras."

The fact that the sense of bodily shame is by no means inborn in mankind is well illustrated by a story told by the owner of a yacht who happened to be cruising in the East. "We were six on board," he writes—"a young married couple, a pretty young widow, and a wealthy Englishman with a very beautiful daughter. One morning Chinese pirates boarded the ship, took us to the coast, and there stripped us of our clothes. Leaving us with bread and water, they locked us in an empty hut and went away, saying that we should regain our clothes and our freedom when they had got a ransom for us. At first we men felt ashamed, but were at the same time curious to see what our ladies looked like undressed. They, however, only showed us their backs. A little later curiosity got the upper hand with them also, and they turned and faced us. Gradually we began to talk naturally, and even indulged in comparisons, jokes, and bold remarks. After four days' captivity embarrassment disappeared altogether, and the absence of clothes worried us no longer. Our eyes and thoughts became accustomed to the new appearance of our lady companions. Their nakedness (although very attractive) ceased to interest us, and seemed less worthy of attention than the dresses by means of which civilization had previously concealed it from us. I then understood why some people see in women's dresses means of sexual excitement. In a week's time we were all living in the happy innocence of the primitives. Finally, we were liberated by the pirates and were given our clothes, and the ladies at once started to dress themselves hurriedly in a corner. When I approached them, I was warned off by the bashful, piercing screams of all three of them. Do you know why? Because they had nothing on but their underwear."

If one considers the theatre as an institution where the supreme longings and ideals of humanity are trying to find their expression in the form of the activity of human beings, where fantasy and intuition oust everyday reality and logic, and where even the most ordinary act of everyday life acquires a new and deeper meaning, for the primitives life in most of its phases was of the theatre. If one understands by acting the transformation of everyday people into imaginary characters, the primitives play-acted in most of the spheres of their existence. Every event in their lives, with the exception of a certain amount of labour, was connected with a ceremony—religious, belligerent, or social—and there was usually a show, a dance or song, as a sign of the celebration. The garments the primitives wore were connected with these theatrical shows and symbolically bound up with them. For them sex was not the objectionable and shameful thing it became later, but was held miraculous and sacred, and most of their religious ceremonies had a sexual foundation, and their ceremonial costumes helped to heighten the attraction of the sexes for each other.

The primitives arrayed themselves with different kinds of ornaments and amulets. The amulets, which were supposed to wield a physical charm, were placed near the sexually attractive parts of the body, while the ornaments were worn in such a manner as to accentuate the architecture and the colouring of the whole body, giving particular significance to its separate forms. The result was merely a fantastically decorated nakedness, all the ornamentation helping the display of the body and the natural expressiveness of its movements. Protective garments such as aprons, loin-cloths, etc., used by some of the Southern primitives for working, hygienic, and other practical purposes, were made and worn by them in a manner forming an harmonious ornamental whole with the rest of their costume, and not as independent bits of clothing.

In contrast the garments of the Northern primitives, such as the Esquimaux, were made merely for utilitarian and protective purposes, and cannot be categorized as costume. Although intrinsically quite picturesque, these garments bear no relation to the proportions of the human figure, their main object being to shield people from the extreme climatic conditions. The body, when clothed in them, becomes transformed into a shapeless bundle of leather, wool, and furs, free and natural movement being rendered impossible.

The costumes of the Antique peoples, who were not handicapped by climatic and moral conditions, were evolved from the ornamentation of the Southern primitives. The idea of a head-dress originated from the primitive head ornaments, worn to make people look taller and to add to their importance. The necklace, worn by the primitives in order to give the neck a longer and slimmer appearance, became the collar, and the ornaments and amulets worn round the hips to accentuate the waist appeared later as the belt, apron, and skirt.

When large pieces of material began to be used by people for ornamentation, these were worn on the same principles as those established by the primitives. The ancient Phœnicians, who were the first great experts at making elaborate heavy materials, used separate specially woven pieces to decorate the upper and lower parts of their bodies. The Phœnicians, who were travelling merchants, sold these woven materials in all parts of the world, and thus their fashions influenced not only the Oriental peoples, but those in most parts of Europe even as far as Brittany. The piece of material used to decorate the torso was woven by the Phœnicians in the shape of a round collar or short cape, and for the lower part of the body they made a kind of apron or used a rectangular piece of material which was wrapped round the waist and hips like a tight skirt, the whole thing being held in place by a belt. The collar and the cape had the effect of accentuating the shape of the neck and the width of the shoulders, while the skirt emphasized the slimness of the waist and the movement of the hips and legs, the ankles being left bare. The part of the torso between the collar and the waist remained uncovered, revealing the chest and the arch of the back. Some of the peoples of Asia Minor, even at the present time, drape themselves in heavy materials, leaving certain parts of their bodies naked, thus accentuating the ornamental value of the draperies and destroying any impression of "covered-up" flesh. (See the picture of the Bedouin girl facing page 8.)

The Egyptians similarly emphasized and even exaggerated the peculiarities of their thin, angular, square-shouldered figures (a type of body which they considered the standard of perfection) by wearing the large round collar and apron-belt. Their women wore the same type of collar and a tight-fitting dress in addition called the "kalasiris," which was often made of transparent material in the shape of a

skirt fastened by a belt or scarf under the breasts or held on the
shoulders by two straps. The kalasiris was either put directly over
the naked body or over additional dresses of a similar pattern worn
underneath.

The female costume of the Cretans, whose civilization was at least
as old as the Egyptian, may seem to us Victorian in style, but it was
quite different from it as far as making and æsthetic principles were
concerned. The Cretan women on the documents appear to wear corsets and short jackets with sleeves reaching to the elbow and bustle-
skirts with flounces, but actually these dresses were made according to
the same principle as those of the Phœnicians. The effect of a narrow
waist was achieved by means of a wide and tight belt, and the skirts,
flounces, and bustle were merely materials so draped as to give this
effect. (See the illustration facing page 20.)

The Greeks, the Etruscans, and the Romans strove to achieve a
similar harmony of bodily form and decoration, although they employed completely different materials from the Egyptians and
Phœnicians. Unlike the heavy quality of the latter, the Greeks,
Etruscans, and Romans used only supple materials for their costumes, draping them round the figure in soft folds. To the Greeks
the usual natural nude was not considered a thing of particular
beauty, but they conceived their gods in terms of perfect specimens
of human beings, and created a standard of perfection for the
human form, into which they sought to transform their own bodies,
and in addition carried these "canons" of the ideal figure into their
sculptures. The Greeks considered that Man should know how to
"wear" his nakedness, and it became for them a costume in itself.
The æsthetic laws, which the Greeks created for the proportions of
the figure, aimed at correcting any individual defects, and the garments
they wore were used to serve this same purpose. Besides cunningly
hiding physical defects with their draperies, the Greek and Roman
women used artifices such as high-soled shoes, false hair, padding

WADSCHAGGA·GIRL

BEDOUIN GIRL

for hips and breasts, make-up, etc., in order to emulate the divine
ideal.

To achieve further the standards of ideal beauty they had created,
the Greeks, Etruscans, Romans, Egyptians, and other cultured peoples
of the Orient attempted to conceal or remove in themselves all traces
of the animal origin of humanity. Thus, for instance, they removed
all hair from the body. The hair of the head and the face was never
left "naturally" dishevelled, as in the "barbarian" manner, but was always arranged decoratively.

The Mediæval costume, and that of subsequent centuries, was
made on quite different principles from that of ancient times. In the
Middle Ages nudity was declared by the Christian religious doctrine
to be shameful. Woman and her body were considered as the instrument of the devil and man as the tempter. Although at that time
men and women washed in a state of nature in the same common
bath-houses, and bathed together in rivers, it would have been considered highly indecent to appear in public with bare arms or legs.
Luxury in costumes became sinful, and people were exhorted to wear
simple clothing hiding the figure. But as vanity and the desire to look
attractive and make a sexual appeal have always been stronger in
mankind than the influence of any moral doctrines, people, especially
women, began to create substitutes for the absence of beautified nakedness. They invented more and more extravagant irrational fashions for
their garments, and devised artful means either of suggesting the hidden forms of their bodies or of exposing some of them or parts of them,
according to the French principle, "cachez un peu ce sein pour que
nous le désirions davantage."

"Si vous jugez," wrote Abel Hermant, "sans parti pris et sans
respect des clichés classiques les modes des siècles les plus réputés
pour leur goût, vous demeurerez d'accord de l'incommodité, de
la disgrace et finalement du ridicule de toutes les toilettes qu'en se
mettant l'imagination à la torture ils ont ordonnées." Since the

Middle Ages, to be rational became absolutely contrary to the essence of what was called "la mode." Beatrice d'Este used to go riding and hunting covered up with masses of jewels in garments most unsuitable for the purpose. The French gentlemen of the time of Louis XVI had to be lifted up in the air by two lackeys to get into their tight-fitting breeches without creasing them. The officers of the First Empire went to fight in uniforms which would choke us if we should wear them now. After the last war women began to wear low-necked and short-skirted dresses with transparent stockings in the streets even during the coldest winter.

After the Middle Ages the figure in its relation to costume began to be considered in its separate parts—the head, the torso, and the lower part, each of these being decorated as a separate item. The tendency to ignore the figure in its entirety led to exaggerated forms of dresses which transformed the wearers into fantastic creatures, their bodies at the mercy of the inventive spirit of the creators of fashions, ceasing to appear natural. The costume of this type, instead of decorating the naked figure, merely formed an intriguing mask for it. The women became "walking dresses" and, as at the present day, their main object was to attract attention to themselves by their extraordinary schemes of decoration, often quite irrelevant to their actual forms.

The men during the Middle Ages, in order to enhance their sexual attraction, began to accentuate the width of the shoulders and the chest and the formation of the leg. It was the bosom, waist, and stomach that were particularly accentuated by the women's dresses at that time, although during divers periods other portions of the figure were emphasized, dresses being made for this especial purpose. This led to the use of artificial devices, which almost deformed certain parts of the women's bodies.

After the Middle Ages, dressed or even in a state of nudity, the women's figures in every period of fashion were very different from what they naturally should be and of course from the Greeks' canons

VENUS OF CYRENE

Museo delle Terme, Rome

Photo by Alinari

for the proportions of physical beauty. Up till now with the dress-makers' art it is not at all necessary for a woman to have a well-built body to be considered beautiful. Being "beautifully dressed," and possessing a face which lends itself to the aid of cosmetics, is quite sufficient to create the desired impression of the moment.

The criterions of feminine beauty changed according to the fashion. Even the artists of the various periods frequently represented the nude beauties in their pictures and sculptures complete with the deformities inflicted upon them by the fashionable costume of the period. How the standard of feminine beauty has altered since the Antique era, and how the conception of physical beauty in general has been influenced by fashion, can be seen by comparing examples of the nude by Greek, Mediæval, and Nineteenth-century artists. The marble Venus from Cyrene, here reproduced, shows what the Antiques imagined to be an ideal body. Their imagination was not influenced by any fashion which deformed the natural human frame. The picture of Eve, by the brothers Van Eyck (facing page 12), shows us, like other Gothic pictures and carvings of nude women, the ideal conception of feminine beauty in the fifteenth century. We can see that Eve's breasts seem to be as if moulded by the bodice of the period, and her waist and protruding abdomen are the products of the high-waisted skirt with folds in front. The statue of Eve (facing page 14) outside the cathedral of Milan, however, belonging to the time (1530-35) when the North Italian woman was not mutilated by fashion, shows us a lady whose body may not have been considered beautiful by the Greeks, but is sufficiently true to nature. The portrait statue of the famous beauty Cléo de Mérode (facing page 16) by the French sculptor Falguière, reflecting the "mode" of the time, shows the kind of female body considered perfect about thirty years ago. The influence of the corset and of the "cache-corset" on the bust, waist, hips and shoulders is clearly visible in that statue.

The shape of woman in 1830 was not at all the same as in 1880, and was again different in 1925, and in none of these years was the figure of woman its natural form. In 1830 and 1880 she was as narrow in the waist as the stem of a liqueur glass. In 1830 the bosom hidden in the corset was full but not over-developed. The lower part of the body hidden by a bell-like skirt was more or less normal. In 1880 the bosom became very full, and the hips and the rump most voluminous, as this was demanded by the new peg-top corset and by the bustle, called by the French "strapontin" or "lieutenant." About 1925 all the marks of femininity disappeared, and the woman was flat-chested and thin-legged like a boy. In 1930 the type of figure "en vogue," as can be seen on the picture of a modern mannequin (facing page 18), was something disproportionately elongated, with a chimney-pot-like neck, arms of extraordinary length, and legs like those of a giraffe.

Of course, every new fashion with its peculiar artificial devices, such as corsets, hoops, bustles, heels, etc., was upsetting to the normal balance of the body and injuriously affected the woman's poise, walk, health and mentality. The walk of a Victorian girl was described as "something between a sideways wriggle and a prance," and the overlaced eighteenth-century ladies were subject to constant "vapours."

As the main object of the Antique costumes was to give full significance to the idealized body, there was little need for a great differentiation between the masculine and feminine attire, and among the peoples of the ancient world it was usually very similar. By the Middle Ages, however, the costumes of men and women had become distinctly removed from each other, and since the twelfth century the forms of feminine dress have developed upon lines completely independent of the male.

In the ninth century the costumes of the men consisted of a short woven tunic, a kind of jacket (called theristrum) which was worn over

ADAM AND EVE

By H. and J. van Eyck
15th Century

From a print by Braun & Co.

a shirt (camisia), and a short cloak which was worn over the tunic. A great deal of attention was paid to the masculine legs, and the young men and warriors set these off by wearing knee breeches and cross-gartered hose or long stockings.

The women, who were not able to expose themselves below the waist, as this was considered by the moralists to be the most objectionable part of them, paid the utmost attention to the upper part of their figures. Their dresses consisted of two tunics—a long one reaching to the ground and worn as a foundation, and a shorter one. In order to give shape to the bosom and waist they wore fitting belts. The sleeves of the lower tunic were worn tight, while those of the over-garment reached to the elbow, and were loose, creating a decorative effect for the arms. Over the tunics a long cloak was worn, and a large veil, covering the head and framing the face, completed the costume.

The women of the eleventh century evolved from their loose robe a gown with long tight sleeves, which fitted the form of the torso and of the arms; they allowed their hair to hang in "silk-broidered" braids. In the thirteenth century, however, they were again exhorted to modesty by the moralists, and were forced to hide their charms more completely. This resulted in the wearing of gorgets or whimples, which concealed the head and the neck, long shirt-like gowns, loose super-tunics, and cloaks of great fullness, the total effect of these garments being reminiscent of a graveyard.

In the middle of the fourteenth century men displayed their legs by wearing tights and very short tunics. In fact, the latter were curtailed to such a degree that they failed even to conceal the cod-piece. The author of the *Chronique de Saint-Denis* wrote as follows in 1370: "La déshonnésteté de vésture et de divers habits, robes si courtes qu'elles ne leur venaient qu-aux fesses, et quand ils se baissaient montraient leurs braies et ce qui était dedans a ceux qui étaient derrière eux et paréillement elles étaient si étroites qu'il leur fallait aide pour les véstir et les déspouiller, et semblait qu'on les écorchait quand on les déspouillait."

The upper part of the woman's tunic in the fourteenth century was worn close-fitting, and the neck was allowed to be exposed. This tight-fitting upper tunic gradually became a separate bodice, and in the fifteenth century the skirt as a separate entity also came into fashion. It grew fuller and fuller, culminating in the stiff farthingale of the Queen Elizabeth period and the Court crinoline of Madame de Pompadour and of Marie Antoinette. In order to balance the abnormal proportions created by the farthingales and crinolines, the women began to wear corked shoes and high heels to add to their stature. These shoes were made tight to make the feet appear small and dainty, and gloves were worn to create a similar effect for the hands.

It was due to the efforts to accentuate the bosom, waist, and hips that the corset was invented in the fifteenth century, its object being to form the foundation for the new exaggerated modes. The corset consisted originally of a bodice, made tight in the waist, which had a piece of wood, looking like a foot-rule or an iron bar, sewn on to the front of it in a vertical position between the breasts. Pieces of tape were attached to the bar, and were tied tightly round the chest. In the sixteenth century the corset was made of metal, and looked like a cone-shaped cage, the costumed body of a woman resembling a "diabolo-top," the lower part being longer than the upper part. The décolleté was firmly established in the fifteenth century. "Par détestable vanité elles font faire leurs robes," says a Frenchman of the time, "si basses a la poitrine et si ouvertes sur les épaules et sur le bas, qu'on voit bien avant dans leur dos, et si étroites qu'a peine peuvent elles dedans respirer, et souventes fois grand douleur y souffrent pour faire le gent corps menu."

The men and women of the latter half of the sixteenth century wore the stiff Spanish dress approved by the Holy Inquisition. The

EVE

Photo by Alinari

Christoforo Solari called il Gobbo
Milan Cathedral.   About 1530-1535

women, being attired in padded bodices—which made the torso look
like an upturned cone—and stiff skirts (vertugales or farthingales),
and leaving none of their natural charms uncovered, attracted the
opposite sex by loading themselves with trinkets and jewels and wearing seductive underwear such as transparent chemises, embroidered
stockings, and elaborate garters. The Venetian courtesans of the sixteenth century wore their stiff skirts (which were cut out in front)
without petticoats, to show their stockinged legs and garters and the
short puffed knickers, and to appear more imposing wore a sort of
cothurnus.

Rabelais, describing the French dress in the reign of François
Ier, says: "Les hommes étaient habillés à leur mode: chausses,
pour les bas d'étamet ou serge drapée en écarlate, migraine blanc
or noir, pour les hauts, de velours, des mêmes ou bien près approchant,
brodés et dechiquetés suivant leur invention, le pourpoint de drap
d'or ou d'argent, de velours, satin, damas, taffetas, des mêmes,
portaient chaussés d'écarlate ou de migraine, et les dites chausses
montaient au-dessus du genou, juste de la hauteur de trois doigts;
et la lisière était de quelques belles broderies ou découpures. Les
jarretières étaient de la couleur de leurs bracelets, et serrées au
genou pardessus et par-dessous. Les souliers, escarpins, et pantoufles,
de velours cramoisi, rouge ou violet, étaient déchiquetés à barbe
d'écrévisse. . . . Par-dessus la chemise, elles (les femmes) vêtaient la
belle vasquine (bodice) de quelques beaux camelots de soie, et sur cette
vasquine vêtaient la vertugale de taffetas blanc, rouge, etc. Au-dessus
la cotte de taffetas d'argent, faite à broderie de fin or, entortillée
à l'aiguille. . . . Les robes, selon la saison, de toile d'or à frisures
d'argent, de satin rouge, etc. En été, quelquefois, au lieu de robes,
elles portaient belles marlottes (cloak with sleeves) des étoffes susdites,
ou des bernes à la mauresque (cloak without sleeves). Et toujours de
beaux panaches selon les couleurs des manchons, bien garni de papil-
lottes d'or. . . . Les patenôtres, anneaux, jazerans, carcans étaient

de fines pierreries. L'accoutrement de la tête était selon le temps: en hiver, à la mode française, au printemps, à l'espagnole, en été, à la turque."

The sixteenth-century Spanish woman's costume, with its corset, bodice, petticoat, and farthingale, served as a prototype for women's fashions from the seventeenth until the last decades of the eighteenth centuries, when the Greek influence began to reassert itself. Because of its theatrically fantastic nature the Spanish sixteenth-century dress was one of the favourite stage costumes, both for men and women, during the seventeenth, eighteenth, and even the nineteenth centuries. It was immortalized by the character of the Capitano in the *Commedia dell' Arte,* and was often worn by the Innamorata of the same Comedy.

In the seventeenth century women began to uncover their arms down from the elbow, and were wearing still lower décolletés than before, exposing the whole bosom, which was frequently forced almost up to the chin by means of special brassières called "gorge-postiches" and "trompeuses" in France. Softer materials were used, but these were still worn over stiff corsets, petticoats, and hoops.

For a short period following the Revolution, the French women, and those of countries which copied the Parisian fashions, began to dress themselves in the manner of the ancient Greeks and Romans. But these Directoire and Consulate fashions did not last long, probably because the women's figures had been ruined to such an extent during the past centuries by the use of corsets, tight belts, garters, and too small shoes with high heels, that it was no longer possible to appear in such a "naturalistic" costume. In the First Empire, Antique dress was worn, only it was made of heavy materials, but soon afterwards the fashions of the sixteenth, seventeenth, and eighteenth centuries began to influence the women again, and the corsets, "cache-corsets," and rows of petticoats came into use.

The women of the nineteenth century started to uncover the

CLÉO DE MÉRODE

The famous beauty of the end of the 19th century
By Falguière

Salon, Paris

1898

upper parts of the arm by wearing only short sleeves, and gradually abolished these in their evening dresses completely, exposing the entire arm, which had been considered highly indecent during the preceding centuries.

There were very few new inventions, with the exception of the bustle skirt, in the other details of the women's toilette during the nineteenth century, the fashions of preceding centuries being varied and adapted for every season of the year.

It was only after the last war that there was a revolutionary change in women's dress due to the new emancipated outlook and interest in sport. The attempt to compete with the male and become independent of him led to a masculine influence in women's clothes. Forgetting their Victorian modesty, the women started to wear soft blouses, without the old corsets, and short skirts without petticoats or even drawers. One of the first people to wage war upon the corset was the famous French couturier, Paul Poiret. He proclaimed the fall of this instrument of torture, which was then called "cache sarraute," and which divided the woman into two separate masses. The so-called brassière was adopted, a kind of bodice which either moulded the breasts or flattened them according to fashion. If in 1900 and before it was considered indecent for a woman to put one leg over another, showing her calves in thick black stockings, in 1925 it became quite natural to expose the legs above the knees in transparent flesh-coloured stockings. In the best circles of English Victorian society it was thought improper even to mention such a thing as a woman's leg. When a big manufacturer expressed to one of the Court officials his desire to present Queen Victoria with twelve pairs of stockings, the official gave him the following dignified reproof: "The Queen of England has no legs, sir." In 1927 women found it quite natural not only to exhibit the lower portion of themselves, but as the French dressmaker Premet said, "d'être nues à leur aise." In 1931 they began to have tea or dinner in the company of men or even walk in the streets in the most revealing pyjamas. Such is the power of fashion over women, and on the evolution of the moral sense. In order to possess the flat, masculine chest decreed by fashion, corsets and brassières of a new shape, often made of rubber, began to be worn like bandages, which pressed the bosom to the chest, with the result that numbers of women now have malformed breasts or no bosom at all. Until the last war and the masculine craze among women, full busts and well-shaped hips and calves were considered marks of beauty, but of late years, by means of artificial devices and dieting, women have reduced these to boyish dimensions. To complete the masculine impression, the wearing of short hair, which up till that time had been considered ugly and objectionable, and even by some people sinful, was declared to be the vogue, and in a very few years most women had cast away many things which had been previously admired as fundamental assets to feminine beauty. Their street or working dresses may have been comfortable to wear, but they were masculine garments, much closer to the idea of clothing than of costume. The women retained some of the feeling for the latter in their evening dresses, although these were merely a combination of some of the details of the elaborate costumes of former times. To compensate for the lack of theatrical spirit in their dresses, the post-war women began to transform even their faces. They began to dye their hair, pluck their eyebrows, took to wearing false eyelashes, and even altered the shapes of their noses, bosoms, hips, and legs by means of surgical operations performed by specialists in "Face and Body Plastics." They used so much make-up that the eighteenth-century actresses, who were notorious for using excessive paint on their faces, would have looked pale and virginal beside them.

The latest women's fashions show a desire to accentuate the natural ease and grace of movement and a tendency to return to femininity, by means of decorating and accentuating the forms of the figure and in the cultivation of the vanished bust, waist, and hair. Most of the

A MANNEQUIN
The 'ideal' figure of a modern woman

inventive spirit of the fashion designers is put into the devising of evening frocks, which are most elaborate garments, showing a combined influence of the Greeks, or rather of the Directoire period, and of the Victorian fashions. The object of these dresses is to expose and to accentuate the body wherever possible. The evening frock of the moment hides very little of the woman above the waist, fits tightly around her hips, and ends with quite a voluminous and long skirt. The bodice, or rather that portion representing the bodice, is often tight-fitting, and in most cases is put directly over the naked body, sometimes even without a "slip." The back is usually lacking.

Men, being normally the attracted and not the attractive, and usually poor in theatrical imagination compared to women, have never altered their physique as the result of costume to such an extent as women, the latter being much more vain. Since the beginning of the nineteenth century, with the growing utilitarian and practical outlook on life, men's costume, which was and still is composed of such items as breeches (modern trousers are merely elongated breeches), waistcoat, and coat, created in the seventeenth century, gradually evolved into *useful* clothing, and in the seventies of the last century became a colourless, dull, traditional civilian uniform entirely lacking in imagination, perhaps a little of it being left in the tail coat of the festive or so-called "evening" dress. Since the War, even military uniforms, in which still lingered the romantic theatrical spirit, have become merely utilitarian garments in most countries.

The theatre, since its early origins, has always been a social reflection of the conditions in which it existed, and of the imaginative susceptibilities of its patrons. Unimaginative rational peoples, incapable of "vision," have no theatre in the *real* sense of the word. The stage of such peoples, representing their superficial lives, reproducing their actions and their conversations, or merely *entertaining* them, is from an artistic and idealistic point of view a senseless, superfluous business. Impulsive peoples, living essentially with the help of the imagination, do not need a theatre as a separate expression of their vision. The primitives were such people, turning every important event of their lives into an imaginative theatrical show. They dressed themselves accordingly, their costumes serving the double purpose of their stage and everyday lives. When, as in Greece, the theatre became a festive ritualistic institution, the dresses of the tragic actors were principally the garments used by the priests. To add to the grandeur and significance of these costumes the Greeks supplemented them with symbolic details, such as masks and cothurni. In the comedies they used grotesque exaggerations of their everyday costumes, supplementing details to accentuate the bestial qualities in people. Until the end of the eighteenth century, while the mode of daily life was romantic, actors did not feel the necessity for wearing costumes in their shows different from those worn in daily life. For them a theatrical performance was in the nature of a festive masquerade, and hence for these performances they simply elaborated their usual fashions. When the actors had to represent some foreign, historical, or allegorical persons, they found it sufficient to add typical or symbolical touches. Mediæval church vestments, which in their origin were nothing more than copies or "stylizations" of ordinary Roman and Byzantine dress, seemed to the Mediæval mind quite imaginative enough to be worn by the heavenly and saintly personages of the Miracle and Morality plays.

Another reason for this wearing of "modern" costumes on the stage was that human beings have always been slaves of traditions, which have created the standard of morals and of so-called "bon ton." Fashions changed very slowly in olden times, and people grew into them. All fixed ideas of respectability and morality had to be uprooted before a woman could appear in a theatrical garb as we understand it now. A seventeenth-century audience, for instance, would

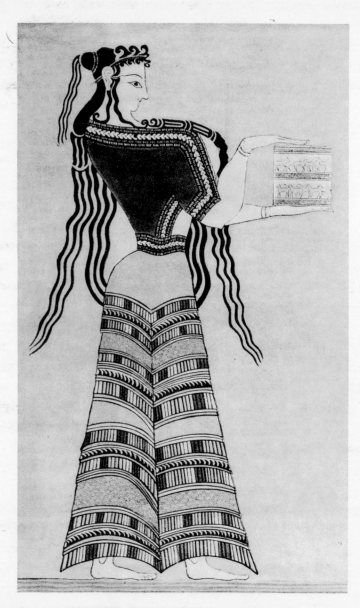

COSTUME OF CRETAN WOMAN

have taken the appearance of a woman dressed in a real Greek tunic at best as a joke and at worst as a scandal.

It was only at the end of the eighteenth century that historical accuracy in costume on the stage began to receive serious attention. Some of the actors tried to introduce "verism" into their stage dresses as early as the seventeenth century, but they did not find any followers. Besides considerations of the necessity for historical truth, interest for the fashions of different periods of history was provoked in the eighteenth century by the fact that fantasy in life gave way at that time to "rationalism," and life costumes began to take less imaginative and picturesque forms. From the end of the eighteenth century historical fashions, rather freely interpreted and combined with contemporary costume, began to be used on the stage. In the fourth decade of the nineteenth century, when the tendencies of the everyday dresses became still less original and interesting, grotesque and exaggerated historical costumes were used on the stage, the nineteenth-century Romantics seeking to divert themselves from prosaic actuality by the poetical elevated emotions of heroic and grotesque stage characters.

Towards the end of the nineteenth century people ceased to be interested in heroics. The fashionable theatres exhibited shows, facsimiles of everyday life, and often served as historical museums for research. Hence imaginative theatrical costume disappeared almost entirely from the majority of the theatres, the dull naturalistic contemporary garments serving adequately for the new rational type of stage show. The historical costumes in the productions of the leading theatres were copied slavishly from museum exhibits. The lesser theatres, directed by people entirely ignorant of the history of costume or even of any theatrical tradition, reproduced historical costume without reference either to historical accuracy or imaginative creation, the resulting concoctions resembling dresses for an impromptu fancy-dress ball.

If it had not been for certain painters, writers, and producing directors, who took a lively interest in the theatre at this time, realizing its vast possibilities, imaginative expressive costume would probably have disappeared from the stage completely. Thanks to these people, called at the time "modernists," there was a revival of *costume* on the stage at the extreme end of the nineteenth and at the beginning of the twentieth centuries, various names such as "stylized," "symbolical," "abstract," "formal," and "mechanical" being given to imaginative creations. The efforts of the modernists, however, have not made any very strong or lasting impression on the stage in general. Their ideas have influenced only a small minority, so-called advanced, while the majority of the so-called commercial theatres still present pre-eminently naturalistic "drawing-room" pieces based on contemporary life, dressing the actors in their uniform suits, and the actresses in the creations of the dressmakers, made mainly for the purpose of advertisement. The actors and actresses partaking in this type of performance are reduced to mannequins, often defeating that very desire for naturalism by their stereotyped costumes. When a commercial director undertakes nowadays to produce what is known as a "costume play," he usually hires the historical dresses from a costumier's shop, or entrusts their making to such a place. Costumes of this type are very often inaccurate historically, and always lack the spirit of the time, the line and the "cachet" of the period. It is almost an impossibility, in this machine age, without spending colossal sums of money and an enormous amount of time, to reproduce the quality of Antique materials and the artificial devices which the wearers used to create the desired effects for the figure. An historical costume which would express the spirit of the period should be *created* by an imaginative artist and not reproduced by a costume maker.

Actors on the modern stage find great difficulty in acclimatizing themselves to the wearing of period or fantastic costume, few of them feeling really at ease even in the tail-coat, the last poor remnant of costume left for civilians nowadays. The women are more adaptable to the wearing of costume than the men, but even so it is very difficult to make a modern actress realize that the eighteenth-century conception of prettiness was not that of a modern chocolate-box designer, and that it is not the few assumed attitudes and mannerisms, copied perhaps from historical pictures, which will make the actress seem "at home" in her costume. Only the association of the character she has to represent with the dress she has to wear and the co-ordination of the movements of her body with those of the dress will make her feel at ease in an historical costume.

Considering the fact that the majority of modern actors and actresses are unhappy wearing period or fantastic costumes on the stage, and that the type of everyday clothes in most cases is dull and uncreative, one might conclude that that which up till now has been known as costume will soon be merely an amusing archaism found only on dusty mannequins in museums. Perhaps its place will be taken in life and on the stage by a type of "uniform" clothing, something like the hygienic and practical working garments by means of which Soviet Russia is seeking to abolish fashion.

However, there is still hope that a resurrection of costume will come from women. It is, perhaps, because of the fact that women are losing the shame of their nakedness and are beginning to feel their bodies that costumes may have a chance to thrive.

But the only hope for men in the matter of costume is to resort to the manner of the German "nudists," and throw all their boiled shirts, starched collars, waistcoats, trousers, braces, etc., to the winds and, taking example from the primitives, start the whole evolution of dress over again.

CHAPTER II

THE GREEK THEATRE

THE Greek theatre originated from religious worship, and was so deeply bound up with it that the rise and fall of the Drama in Greece coincided with the popularity of the reigning gods. It was at its height when belief in the gods was unimpaired, and decayed when this belief began to weaken and public worship to decline. Eight hundred years lie between its first and last "curtains."

The original function of the Greek performances was propaganda for religion, as later were the performances of the Miracle Plays of the Middle Ages. The gods and their companions were brought before the eyes of believers in order to strength reverence and faith. The Greek religious festivals of theatrical nature were principally connected with the worship of Dionysus. The myth of that god was associated with the death of nature in the autumn, its rebirth in the spring, and with the constant cycles of transition from grief to joy in all living things. In Athens theatrical festivals took place during those days which were held sacred to Dionysus. There were celebrations which were held by the country folk around Athens in the month of Poseidon (December-January) called Rural Dionysia, and in Gamelion (January-February) there were further celebrations in one of the districts of Athens called Lenæa. In the city itself the Dionysia were held in the month of Elaphebolion (March-April). At the festivals of Dionysus crowds sang and danced round the flaming altar to the accompaniment of instrumental music. In these shows the arts of poetry, music, and dance were rhythmically united, leading to an entirely new kind of art—the art of the theatre. Pindar and his contemporaries composed songs for these dances ("dithyrambus," i.e. song of the goat), which were sung by a chorus, the members of which were dressed in goat-skins, this animal being sacred to Dionysus. Between the songs the leaders of the chorus explained the meaning and significance of the verses, and later on, about 534 B.C., a costumed spokesman appeared. He was introduced, as the legend goes, by Thespis, whom the Greeks considered as the founder of their theatre. As the leader and producer of a company of besmeared, strolling singers and dancers, Thespis wandered with them throughout Greece on a chariot, taking the part of the spokesman in their performances. Later it became customary for the poet-dramatist himself to appear in this part, and it was also his business to train and rehearse the chorus in song and dance. What was known as dialogue evolved from the exchange of speech between the spokesman and the leaders of the chorus.

The first step towards the Drama having thus been taken, the way lay open for many varieties of dramatic activity, including Tragedy and Comedy. The former was dedicated to the gods and providence, the latter to the activities and strivings of their unruly adherents and followers. The development inaugurated by Thespis proceeded quickly. At the time of the battle of Marathon, according to Aristotle, Æschylus introduced a second spokesman, and by so doing showed that the birth of real Drama was at hand; whereupon the scene of action promptly shifted. If, up till now, dancing round altars had sufficed for these productions, it now became necessary that the two spokesmen, while facing each other, should be seen by the whole audience. Regard for acoustics necessitated the introduction of a background, and the spokesmen appeared before a wall or screen, so that the former round arena of the festival contracted to the semicircle of the theatre. It was closed in by the introduction of a raised stage. Æschylus's successor, Sophocles, added a third spokesman to the second, and this trio of actors, Protagonist, Deuteragonist, and Tritagonist, was never added to. The Greek Tragedy was limited to these three, and even if Sophocles' contemporary, Euripides, made technical improvements in stage-craft, he made no fundamental changes in the Greek Drama.

The function of the Greek Tragedy was not to present a picture of life and its various conflicts and problems, but, in those realms of thought which it represented, to serve as the highest expression of the Dionysian festivals. It was based on ideals, was imbued with a spirit of dignity and solemnity, and took for its subjects the legends of mythology and its characters from among the gods and heroes. Thus Greek tragic theatrical productions were not merely for the purpose of amusement and pleasure, but were religious celebrations in honour of divinity. The Greek tragic theatre was not an entertainment, but a school of religion and a place of worship, where homage was rendered to the gods in the name of the whole nation. As religion in Greece was the affair of the State, so too the theatre was entrusted to the care of the State authorities, and it was the duty of the rich citizens of Athens to provide the chorus and to bear its expense. Entrance to the theatre was free. The State was also responsible for the staging of the production, and had to provide (since the time of Sophocles) the three actors for each production. About 456 B.C. the State started competitions for actors similar to those which existed for sport or arts.

As the result of never allowing more than three *speaking* characters on the stage at the same time, supers were introduced in the performances of Greek Tragedy. During the course of the play these had to act the most varied dumb rôles. The limited scope to which Greek Drama was confined by the restriction of the number of speaking rôles sometimes forced playwrights to reduce the important characters to dumb mannequins during parts of the play. Furthermore, they had to consider the perpetual changes of costume from the actors to the supers and vice versa. In Euripides' *Orestes,* Pylades, who does not utter a word during the whole of the last act, was played by a super in this act, as there were already three speaking characters on the stage in the persons of Orestes, Menelaus, and Apollo, and the actor who played Pylades in the speaking parts was required for one of these characters. Alongside the dumb Pylades were the silent Electra and Hermione, all three of whom were also played by supers. Similarly in Sophocles' *Ajax,* Tekmessa, who up to a certain moment takes a lively part in the dialogue, suddenly becomes a silent character. In many other Tragedies the same part in the same show had to be played by several performers.

The Greek chorus in Tragedy, according to Pollus, until the production of Æschylus' *Eumenides,* was composed of fifty people, while others assert that it did not number more than twelve or fifteen. In the Satyr-play (of which I write later) the chorus at first numbered twelve, but later it increased to fifteen. Ancient Comedy had a chorus of twenty-four. Gradually the rôle of the chorus diminished in importance, and it seems that 317 B.C. saw the end of it.

The Greek actors, impersonating the tragic dramatis personæ from the realms of gods and heroes, wore costumes which made them look superhuman, increasing their height and width. Masks, shoes with raised soles, and padding on the body distinguished them from chorus and audience alike. Even before the actors uttered a word, people in the audience could see that they were not meant to represent ordinary human beings. In addition to high shoes the tragedian was padded on the chest and back, the paddings being known as *progastridion* and *prosternidion,* and probably a means was even found for strengthening and lengthening the arms. Over this padding they put a kind of knitted vest (*somation*), and only over this the actual costume was worn. The tragedies of Æschylus were acted in a costume which dated from the time of Thespis. It was the long dress of the priests of Dionysus, and has sometimes been affirmed to be that of the god himself. It was very rich and colourful, and was of Asiatic origin. The tragedies of Sophocles and Euripides were played in apparel belonging to more than two generations previous. The brightly coloured and richly decorated Ionian costumes were worn by the Greeks in private life until the Persian Wars, and only later they changed them for the more simple Dorian dresses. The luxurious Ionian dresses, however, continued to be worn by musicians and actors, remaining conventional stage costumes. The same Ionian fashions were used for the characters of both men and women (which were of course played by men).

There was no difference in principle between Greek male and female dress. Some minor additions, such as veils, were sometimes worn by women, but the essentials of the male and female dress consisted of two garments, either or both of which could form the costume, and which correspond roughly to shirt and mantle.

In many cases both the upper and the under garment were rectangular pieces of material folded round the body, and held in their place either by the movements of the wearer or by temporary fastenings. Except in certain rare and exceptional cases, all the forms of Greek dress can be produced without the aid either of scissors or of needle and thread.

The mantle varied in size, and was worn in many different fashions, enveloping the whole or only part of the person. At times it was merely draped, at others fastened with a brooch of some kind. In one of its forms, the *chlamys* (a military cloak affected especially by youths), it was quite small, and was clasped on the shoulder or at the neck. The ampler mantle worn by elderly men and women (often called *himation*) was large enough to envelop the person completely. It was generally worn unbrooched. Men often wore the himation alone, but the women were obliged to wear the tunic underneath.

The tunic, called the chiton, although worn over the naked body, must not be regarded merely as underwear. It was intended in itself to serve all the purposes of dress, save where special protection of the person was desired. It could be coloured and artistically adorned, had showy fastenings, and was completed and rendered serviceable by a girdle. There were two distinct kinds of tunics. One, made of thick material falling into large folds, was worn short and without sleeves or any covering for the arms, and was sometimes open on one side. The other, draped into multitudinous crinkly folds, was made of a thin fabric of ample dimensions. It descended below the feet and covered the arm, or the upper part of it, with a full sleeve. A girdle was sometimes worn with either dress, and in addition the latter kind was sometimes secured over the bust and under the arms by secondary bands. The one tunic was usually of a woollen material, the other of a fine linen or cotton fabric, and they appeared generally to answer to the traditional distinction which archæologists have drawn between the Doric and the Ionian tunics.

Some people think that, while the Dorian tunic was merely draped round the figure, the Ionic garment was shaped and sewn. Experiments, however, made with actual drapery show that there are several ways of fastening the Ionic tunic and its sleeves, that do not require the use of needle or thread.

The material of the Greek dress worn by ordinary people was simple and cheap, and in many cases was the product of the household loom. It could be dyed, especially when it was of wool, any desired colour, and be decked with a figured border woven into the fabric. The evenly woven soft web of fine wool or flax was taught to fall with a lovely play of lines assisting the expression of the form of the body beneath.

In contrast to the indiscriminately coloured dress which was worn in everyday life, that of the tragic actors was of bright colours and richly decorated. The chiton was either embroidered with ornaments or figures of people and animals, or of both, or had stripes and other patterns on it. In the fifth century the ornaments on the stage dresses became most elaborate, and even pieces of precious metal were used for decorative purposes. The chlamys was heavily decorated with gold embroideries, and the bright chiton known as the *poikilon* was ornamented with coloured figures clearly outlined on a light background. Those in distress and the exiled wore costumes of rough materials and of dark colours (grey, mustard yellow, blue, and black). People in mourning wore black and sometimes plain white. Queens were arrayed in a flowing purple dress with a train, or a white robe with purple edge, or with two purple stripes running along the hem, and in a white purple-edged cloak. Grief-stricken queens wore black with a train, and a blue or apple-green shawl. Women, apart from queens, wore red, in Euripides' time white, and, as Pollux says, purple. Huntsmen and soldiers wore the purple chlamys, and kings wore a green cloak and the long *kolpoma,* which was put on over the poikilon and, according to some, was similar to the chiton and had sleeves. In addition to these conventional clothes there were other stage garments peculiar to certain classes and professions. A unique garment seems to have been the *agrenon,* described as a shawl, and worn by seers and soothsayers. This was of closely knit wool and covered the whole figure. It was worn by Cassandra and other prophetesses.

In cases where the costume was not sufficiently individual, certain attributes were used in order to accentuate the character. The head-dress may be included among the accessories to stage costume. Pallas Athene was distinguished by the ægis, Thanatos carried a sword, as did Ulysses, Orestes, Menelaus, and others. Kings carried a sceptre with an eagle at the top, priests had staffs wreathed in laurel, old men long sticks to aid them in walking. A wreath on the head signified a festive, exalted, or honourable condition. Those imploring aid carried twigs bound with wool. Travellers were recognizable by wearing hats, as may be seen, for example, in the cases of Orestes and Pylades and the retinue in the *Choephoræ* of Æschylus. Women had, according to Pollux, bonnets, fillets, and veils on their heads, and wore the pallium draped over the back of the head.

One of the most essential features of the dress of a tragic actor was the *cothurnus*. "Kothornos" was originally the name of the square shoe for women from which stage footwear was adopted. The stage cothurnus, with a very high sole, came into existence very late, and is only to be found in the time of the Roman Emperors. In the most ancient times the stage cothurnus was nothing more than the leg-boot of Dionysus, which, like the costume of the god, was of Asiatic origin, and which had been introduced on to the stage along with his robes. This leg-boot of soft leather seems to have possessed a more stocking-like character at the time of Thespis, and only received a stiff sole in the time of Æschylus, which, however, does not seem to have been very thick. It was then a high boot with turned-over scalloped flaps at the top and had a slit in front which was laced together cross-wise. In the fifth century B.C. its chief characteristic was not the high sole, but the high leg decorated with a palm-leaf ornament. Gradually the sole became thicker and thicker, and this was eventually the main difference between the cothurnus and ordinary footwear. At first the sole was raised by layers of leather, but later wood was used. This was in the second century B.C., when the boot came half-way up the leg and was not only coloured as in the first century, but completely gilded. At the time of the early Roman Emperors, when the boot was concealed by the chiton, it had become such a high and clumsy stilt, that anyone who fell on the stage when wearing these stilt-boots could not get up without assistance.

The chorus in Greek Tragedy was dressed, like the actors, with great lavishness. Demosthenes once produced a male chorus of flute players clad in gold brocade and gold wreaths. The tragic chorus wore masks like the actors, but differed as regards their costume. They did not wear cothurni, as they had to dance, and were similarly prevented by their dancing from wearing long dresses. They were clad in various shorter garments which did not much differ from the chiton and himation worn in everyday life. The members of a chorus were all dressed alike, unless, in certain circumstances, special modifications in costume were necessary to the action of the play.

It was very different, however, when non-Greeks appeared, or when the chorus had to suggest a supernatural atmosphere. Such situations naturally called for a certain fantasy and "couleur locale" in the costume. The revengeful Eumenides, for instance, appeared dressed all in black with snakes in their dishevelled hair.

If the reproduction of an actual event was presented before an Athenian audience, such as, for instance, *The Fall of Miletus* of Phrynichos, or *The Victory of Salamis* of Æschylus, the producer dressed the play so as to differentiate between the Greeks and the foreigners. It is even not improbable that on these occasions the audience was regaled with the sight of the actual booty and spoil in general, which the victorious Persian Wars had brought to Greece. People like Persians, Thracians, Egyptians, and other Orientals appeared in different dress from Greeks, and even a black and coloured make-up was used for the bodies of the members of the chorus.

In this attempt to evolve a typical costume may be discerned the beginning of a reaction against the conventional stage-costume of the tragic actor, and a tendency towards the introduction of more naturalistic dresses on the stage. In *The Persians* Æschylus makes the Queen Atossa, on hearing the news of the destruction of the Persian Army by the Greeks, take off her regal attire and reappear in ordinary clothes. In the last scene of this tragedy the conquered Xerxes is shown in tattered kingly robes, torn in grief and anger. In the tragedies of Euripides, refugees or unfortunates like Jocasta and Electra also appeared in torn garments, and Sophocles wishes his Philostetes and Telephas to come on in torn, and Œdipus in dirty, unkempt garments. He goes even farther than Euripides, when he makes Hercules disrobe before his son to show him how the shirt of Deianira has burnt his flesh.

GREEK ACTORS

Apart from the tragic chorus there was also the chorus of satyrs in the comic sequel to the Tragedy known as the Satyr-play. This Satyr-play was not only rough comedy, but almost always coarsely sensual. Æschylus, Sophocles, and Euripides wrote for this "genre." In the Satyr-comedy the actor wore the long rich robe of the god Dionysus and his priests, while the chorus appeared in the likeness of centaurs and satyrs, the horse or goat-like companions of the god, creatures who were half demons, half animals. On the Satyr Vase at Naples, painted about 400 B.C., are seen the actors and the chorus of Satyr-comedy before the beginning of the show. The actors are dressed in the magnificent robes customary to Tragedy, and the members of the chorus are wearing loin bandages made of goatskins to which are attached upstanding *phalluses* of red leather—the symbol of the procreative power of Dionysus. Rams', stags', and panthers' skins were worn by the satyrs also, but, as the latter were very rare, they had to be imitated by artificial means. In later times goats were supplanted by horse demons (centaurs). The centaurs wore horses' ears and tails.

The Greek tragic theatre, disdaining the vital aspirations and ideals of the masses, and remaining a conservatively religious institution, gradually lost touch with life, and therefore failed in time to interest and attract people. Already in *The Frogs* Aristophanes makes Hercules laugh at the absurd dress of Dionysus, and finally in Lucian's time, Tragedy was merely considered as something with which to frighten children. Greek Comedy, on the other hand, had always kept pace with the times, and although it began with all the paraphernalia of its religious origin, it dropped these ostentations when they no longer appealed to the taste of later generations.

The Ancient Greek Comedy, known as the Old Attic Comedy, was originally connected with the gay side of the cult of Dionysus, from which it took the characters of the phallus-wearing dancers. The phallus influenced the themes of this Comedy, and the sexual

relations were the most important subject of fun. The most flourishing period of the Old Attic Comedy is represented by Aristophanes
(454-404 B.C.), and its character was reflected by the dress in which
it was played.

The men's costume in Comedy was always furnished with the
phallus of red leather used for comic "business." It has been doubted
by some specialists on this matter whether actors wore the phallus in
Aristophanes' day, but there are passages in his plays which clearly
indicate that this was the case. In the scene between Kinesias and
Myrine in *Lysistrata* the exposed phallus plays an important part. It
was used on the stage as long as there was any connection between
the play and the religious cult, and it was banned from the theatre at
the end of the fifth century. The popular strolling actors, however,
the Mimes, not only wore the phallus long before Attic Comedy came
into existence, but also long after it had ceased, in fact right up to
the decline of the Byzantine Empire.

An outstanding feature of the costume of Old Attic Comedy was
the comic padding of the body, intended to provoke laughter like the
comic costume of our circus clowns. The stomach and the actor's
posterior were both heavily padded. Over these was worn a vest
made of stretchable stuff on which nipples and navel were painted.
The usual colour of this garment was flesh-tint, or red, reddish brown,
and yellow. Sometimes it had a pattern of diagonal stripes, sometimes
arms and legs were covered with vertical and intermixed with diagonal
stripes. These may have been intended to represent tattooing, which
may be traced to the most ancient times.

Over the paddings and the vest the actual costume was worn.
Comedy, unlike Tragedy, had no special costume of its own. The
actors wore everyday dress which, however, was caricatured. Both
chiton and mantle were unusually short, so that the phallus should
always remain visible. People of low standing wore clothes of shoddy
or worn-out material, and slaves wore leather jerkins or skins.

The chlamys was only worn on the stage by those of whom it was characteristic, i.e. warriors—among others, the Spartans in *Lysistrata*.

In contrast to Tragedy, the comic theatre emphasized the difference between the sexes in the matter of clothes. Women of the upper classes wore the long chiton with a girdle round the waist and a himation with an embroidered edge. The short chiton was used by the servants and by all the members of the lower orders. Women also wore the frontal and back paddings.

The colour of the clothing was important in the comic theatre inasmuch as certain colours signified sex, age, and social standing. This was even more noticeable in the New Attic Comedy. In the Old Comedy the women's dress seems to have been white, pale blue, and saffron yellow. The old women in the sacrificial scene in *Pluto* wore gay-coloured clothing. The white dress was characteristic of young girls, while very bright clothing was a sign of wealthy people or of prostitutes. Young men always appeared bareheaded, unless they were travellers. Old men and slaves wore caps. Women wore hoods or fillets round the hair. Ankle shoes, often mentioned by Aristophanes, were worn by men, and by women the cothurnus, which was high in the leg and had square soles. The paintings on Apuleian vases belonging to the third century B.C. and terra-cotta figures from Athens, Tanagra, etc., give us an idea of the costumes, masks, and of the grotesque sense of humour of the comic actor of the Old Attic Comedy.

The chorus of the Old Comedy, like the actors, when representing ordinary people wore a caricature of everyday dress. They often had to appear as fantastic, allegorical, mythological, and animal figures, such as clouds, towns, isles, sphinxes, sirens, wasps, frogs, birds, etc. When representing clouds the members of the chorus appeared in bright, loose-floating garments, and wore long noses. The costumes of animals were only suggested, and the human figure was never completely hidden by them. The costume of the birds in

Aristophanes' comedy of the same name consisted of tights which were decorated with feathers. A pair of wings were fixed to the arms. The wasps were symbolized by the narrow waist and the sting. The horsemen in another comedy of the same writer wore helmets and tight-fitting striped vests over sleeveless tunics. They sat on the shoulders of men representing horses. The latter had thick tails fixed to the padding of their posteriors, and wore horses' heads.

The New Attic Comedy was of a different character from its predecessor, and therefore differed in the matter of costume. Its chief exponent was Menander, 342-291 B.C., and it chose for its subjects incidents from private life. The society it depicted consisted of a variety of characters. The New Attic Comedy had no relationship with religion, had inherited nothing from the old theatrical wardrobe, and had banned the chief feature of the costume of Ancient Comedy, the phallus. It also ceased to pad the body, since, as there was no longer such a demand for lewdness and coarse jokes, there was no more use for these costume effects. It found its chief interest in the action and in the types, not in obscenity. Its characters were the contemporaries of the spectators who shared their weaknesses and wore the same clothes. Although the under-vest was retained, it was no longer grotesquely padded, and the garments worn over it show no peculiarities of cut to distinguish them from the citizens' daily dress. The men wore the chiton, the different lengths of which signified social standing. The outer garment of the men was the himation—which had a fringe when worn by people of distinction —though soldiers and servants wore the chlamys. Slaves are often depicted only in a short smock girded at the hips, open on the left side of the chest and with a sleeve for the right arm. The men's chiton was either sleeveless or had sleeves which varied a good deal in length and width. The women's dress consisted of a chiton reaching to the feet, with sometimes a coloured hem, and the himation, which in the case of heiresses had a fringe, but which was not worn by women of the lower classes. The colour of the clothes seems to have remained the same as before. Boys dressed in purple, men in brown, and old age in white. Parasites and toadies wore black or grey; slaves white, and eunuchs striped materials. Young women wore white, old ones green or sky-blue, prostitutes wore multi-coloured dresses. Some pictures show people wearing a variety of colours, men in purple chiton with red himation, or brown and violet chiton with blue himation, or blue chiton and dark-blue himation. An old man is represented in a long-sleeved white cloak with fringes, a soldier in white chiton and purple chlamys. One can see women dressed in light-green chitons with scarlet or yellow himation, others in green chitons with dark-green hems and yellow cloaks with narrow violet edges, a procuress in light-green chiton, scarlet cloak, red hood, and yellow shoes. A female slave is depicted in a chiton striped in red, black, and blue. The head was nearly always uncovered, as in daily life, but soldiers wore a round hat which was inseparable from the chlamys. Women wore fillets, wreaths, and diadems. Old men carried crooks and country folk staffs. Ankle shoes or sandals were worn, which were yellow, red or grey in colour. Social differences do not seem to have been more emphasized by clothes on the stage than off. The skin-coat or leather smock became the typical dress for peasants in Comedy, with the pilos or pointed felt hat.

The Greeks were always more concerned with presenting ideas in art rather than individuals, and peopled their tragic as well as comic theatres with types—not persons. Inasmuch as this is true, the use of masks by Greek actors becomes understandable, and in fact it has advantages when it is remembered that women's rôles were played by men. Also characters of any age could be played in masks by any actor. Furthermore, owing to the size of the ancient theatres, the "mimique" was not so noticeable as it is to-day, and masks with strongly marked exaggerated features were certain of making a striking impression on the audience. The mask's function was to impress and plastically to present the typical character, and to do away with the variations of passing moods, and it may well be doubted whether the characters of Ancient Tragedy would have achieved their grandeur without the impression and the restraint imposed by the mask.

One great advantage arising from the use of masks was that they gave no scope to personal vanity on the part of actors, and saved the Greek theatre from that glamour of "personality" which is one of the curses of the modern theatre.

The custom of wearing masks on the Greek stage came from the ancient phallus-wearing comic singers and dancers, who from decency covered their faces. In very ancient times they wreathed their faces with leaves and coloured them with soot, lees of wine, or the sap of plants. The invention of the actual masks, as with everything concerning the theatre, was attributed by the Greeks to Thespis, and originally they were made only of canvas. One of the reasons why the mask remained in use on the Greek stage long after the religious origin of the custom had been forgotten was probably the Greek sense of modesty. To appear on the stage without a mask was almost an outrage. Demosthenes called Kyrebion an infamous wretch because he dared to take part in a public procession of a religious nature without a mask.

The Greek mask not merely covered the face, but went over the whole head. Since the time of Æschylus it was made of leather, plastered wood, etc., and was so heavy that the wearer had to protect his head with a felt cap. The actor saw through the pupils of the eyes of the mask and spoke through an opening in its mouth. The opening for the mouth, sometimes very wide, is frequently shown as funnel-shaped; the reason for this has not been adequately explained. The assumption that it acted as the funnel of a trumpet or a megaphone to strengthen the voice will hardly hold good, as masks so constructed belong only to a late period.

Pollux, who lived in the second half of the second century A.D., has left in his *Onomasticon* a catalogue of a stock of masks used by a troupe of actors. He enumerates 44 characteristic men's masks (17 tragic and 27 comic), and 25 female masks (8 tragic and 17 comic). Pollux classifies the masks according to the physical qualities, the social standing, and the nationality of the character. He mentions masks of a girl, a cropped girl, a withered old woman, a fat old woman, a curly-headed young man, a fair-haired man, a pointed-bearded man, a long-bearded old man, a beardless satyr, a grey-haired satyr, Father Silenus, an overripe prostitute, an old woman house-keeper, a hairy lady's-maid, a gossiping woman, a young peasant, an industrious young man, a young Sicilian, etc.

At a later period the masks were specified according to age, temperament, mood, and also complexion, hair, and beard. The complexion of the mask was a very important character feature. The women's masks were white and the men's brownish. A hooked nose was a sign of impudence, and was an attribute of the parasite, a snub nose was the hall-mark of the yokel and old housekeeper. The eyes of the masks were objects of great importance for purposes of characterization, as is shown by the remarks of Pollux, who speaks of sad, painful, gloomy, ill-tempered, piercing, languid, squinting, and other glances. In order to reproduce these in the mask the iris must of necessity have been part of the mask. The eyebrows were also specially marked in different characters. The colour of the hair and the shape of the coiffure was also a distinguishing mark. Fair hair was considered particularly beautiful. A "knob" of hair above the forehead with a falling curl, known as the *onkos*, the invention of which was attributed to Æschylus, was worn by women and young men. The fringe was worn by kings in Tragedy and by soldiers in Comedy. In general, there does not seem to have been much difference between the hair on male and female masks. There were masks with ringlets worn by young men as well as by women in the parts of prostitutes. Closely cropped hair was a sign of mourning in both sexes. A bald head was found only on comic masks, and worn by the procurer, the cook, the foreign slave, etc. Mature manhood and the approach of old age was always signified by a beard. The same hero appeared in a different mask, not only in each play, but often he wore different masks in different scenes of the same play, in order to suit other situations and moods.

It seems as if Æschylus had thought about a change of mask during the performance even in his time. In his last work, *Oresteia,* Clytemnestra appears after the murder of Agamemnon with blood on her forehead. The actor playing Clytemnestra must have changed his mask behind the scenes to produce this effect. In Sophocles a change of masks is quite plainly to be traced. It is certain that Œdipus, after his blinding, appeared in another mask. In Euripides a change of mask seems to have been as frequent as a change of costume, which this writer took special pains to effect. In the blinding of the Cyclops he obtained the most horrifying effect by giving to those blinded masks empty eye sockets streaming with blood, which obviously necessitated a change of masks. As the tragic chorus remained on the stage throughout the play a change of masks by its members is improbable, or at least was limited to exceptional circumstances.

It is safe to assume that the difference between the masks of the Greek theatre in the earlier times and those of the later period was as great as the difference in the plastic art in general. Some authorities declare that the masks express the general standard of Greek art of their time. It is probable that the masks of Æschylus' tragedies were more grotesque and impressive than those worn in Sophocles' plays, and that those in Euripides were of a more realistic type, as the result of that poet's predilection for realism which he had already shown in the matter of costumes.

The masks of the Ancient Greek Comedy generally aimed at caricaturing the human face in general. They exaggerated and distorted it in the direction of ugliness and the comic, and attempted to turn the human countenance into that of some animal. The New Attic Comedy, which was concerned with the private lives of individuals and had evolved a regular stock of stereotyped types, expressed them in the masks, which were worn again and again in all the plays. The ancient Greek Comedy did not refrain from representing living persons, or those lately dead, on the stage, and calling them by their actual names. Thus, after Pericles' death, Eupolis put Solon, Miltiades, Aristides, and Pericles; Aristophanes put Socrates on the stage, Euripides put Cleon, and we have every reason to suppose that the masks worn were actual portraits of those people they represented. In *The Knights* of Aristophanes, Demosthenes, before Cleon's entrance, tells the audience that no mask-maker would mould Cleon's mask through fear of that demagogue. Platonius assures us that portrait masks were worn in Comedy, and we know that Socrates, at a performance of *The Clouds,* stood up before the public so that they might compare him with the mask of himself which was being worn on the stage. These portrait-masks were most certainly caricatures, as were the characters in the plays. The comedies of Aristophanes are particularly rich in fine masks. The chorus in *The Clouds* had large misshapen noses, and the chorus of the frogs wore masks with gaping mouths.

CHAPTER III

THE ROMAN THEATRE

I N Rome a theatrical performance, though always a feature of religious festivals, was only superficially related to religion. It was regarded merely as a pleasant diversion or function whereby the triumph of a victorious general, for instance, might be celebrated, or the opening of an important public building be consecrated. The theme of the show, however, would have nothing to do with the attendant event.

The tragic theatrical productions in Rome, because of the Roman taste for luxury and extravagance, developed into displays of the most costly and ostentatious dresses and spectacles. Horace describes some of these shows in which cavalry exercises were performed on the stage, and in which giraffes and elephants appeared. In the tragedy *Clytemnestra* 500 mules bore the booty of Agamemnon, and the Trojan Horse contained 3,000 vessels. Nero, in the course of his reign, gave about 2,200 million sesterces to actors and athletes. Neither he nor his successors spared any expense or trouble to attain at least the most blatant realism. According to Suetonius, Nero had a real house set on fire in one play, and another emperor ordered the captured leader of a band of robbers to act the principal part in a play which ended by his being bound to a cross and actually torn to pieces by wild beasts.

The theatre in Rome was not, as in Greece, a State institution, but was run by private individuals. The Greek theatre was essentially national, born of the Greek spirit on Greek soil, whereas that of Rome was something that had been imported from abroad.

Theatrical productions were unknown to the Romans until 364 B.C., although games in the circus were indulged in by them from their earliest history. The first theatrical shows which were given in Rome consisted of dancing to the accompaniment of flutes, and were brought from Etruria. The young Roman patricians began to imitate these dances and the rustic farcical performances of strolling Oscan players in their amateur shows. The performances of these strolling players were known as the Atellanæ, named after the place of origin, Atella in the Roman Campagna. The Atellanæ were played in the Oscan tongue "al improvviso," and consisted mostly of rough popular humour, parody, satire, acrobatics, pantomime, and clownish buffoonery. The Atellanæ took their material mostly from the life of the lower classes, and represented other stratas of life and people from the point of view of these classes. The principal dramatis personæ of the Atellanæ were limited to five "permanent" types. These were Maccus, Bucco, Pappus, Dossenus, and Manducus, who appeared in the guises of peasants, servants, doctors, soothsayers, procurers, soldiers, pedagogues, philosophers, and others. The first was a sensual, stupid, impertinent, and witty coward. Bucco had a self-satisfied, boastful, and silly nature, and in addition was a glutton and a thief. Pappus was a lecherous old miser, and Dossenus was a cunning and boastful chap, with many characteristics in common with Pappus. The ogre Manducus evolved in the comedies of Plautus as the Miles Gloriosus, and was transformed into the bombastic swaggering Capitano by the Italian *Commedia dell' Arte*. Besides these characters Lamia the Ghoul also appeared in the Atellanæ, representing the patron of all schemers. The characters of the Atellanæ were for a long time identified by certain authorities with the types of the Italian *Commedia dell' Arte,* Arlecchino corresponding to Maccus, Brighella to Bucco, Pulcinella to Maccus and Bucco, Pantalone to Pappus, and the Dottore to Dossenus. The Atellanæ were played in masks which were tight-fitting, unchanging, and inseparable from the permanent types of the dramatis personæ. In Rome the wearing of masks was originally a privilege permitted only to young men of noble birth, who, however, acted in farcical plays taken from the Atellanæ. It is impossible to say whether the masks, which were part and parcel of the general outfit of the Atellanæ, were actually of Oscan origin or Greek. They may well have come into existence in Italy as they did in Greece, i.e. as the result of painting and disguising the face. We know from Tibullus and Virgil that painting the face with chrome yellow and soot, and the use of cork masks, were old customs in Italy. Different types of animals seem to have been chosen as the basis for the physiognomies presented by the masks of the Atellanæ. The farcical shows derived from the Atellanæ were greatly "en vogue" in Rome at the time of Sulla, but in Julius Cæsar's and Cicero's time they had been ousted by mime.

It was only in 240 B.C. that the Romans, through a Greek slave, became acquainted with tragedy and regular comedy. In that year Livius Andronicus, a Greek from Tarentum, produced the first Roman tragedy and the first Roman comedy. The Roman writers of tragedies began by following the Greek models, and the Roman writers of comedies produced plays in the Latin tongue but in the Greek spirit and in the style of Menander. The two most celebrated Romans who wrote comedies in the Greek manner were Plautus and Terence.

Besides the imitations from the Greek, there were national tragedies in Rome and national comedies. The actors wore the Grecian dress in tragedies and comedies taken from the Greek, and retained in their national tragedies the Greek cothurnus and the long rich garments of the kings to which they added other national Roman garments, including the *toga*. The essential parts of the Roman national costume were the *toga,* the *tunic,* the *stola,* and the *palla*.

The *toga* was originally worn by Roman priests at sacrificial celebrations, but later it became an accepted costume for honourable citizens in everyday life. The toga consisted of a piece of material three times the height of a man in length and twice his height in width.

The forms of this garment varied, round pieces of material sometimes being used. In order to drape themselves in the toga, the Romans began by folding the material near the middle of the length, and placed it on the left shoulder. Public officials wore white togas (Toga candida), the Toga prætextata was worn by priests and kings, and was decorated with a purple band. The Toga picta, made of purple material embroidered with gold, was worn only by victorious generals, and the Toga sordida was worn by those accused of crime. The tunic was worn underneath the toga and acted as an indoor dress for men. It resembled a large shirt with or without sleeves, and was worn with a belt. In Rome only a foreigner would dare to appear in the street wearing trousers, which were of Oriental origin. During cold weather the Romans bound their legs with bands similar to puttees, only soldiers being allowed to wear knickers down to the knee, which later were transformed into trousers. The Roman women wore a tunic with long or short sleeves directly over the naked body. This was originally made of wool, but later cotton, silk and even transparent gauze were used, and a belt was worn with it. Towards the end of the Roman Empire, the tunic had acquired a train and sleeves decorated with buttons. Over the tunic the women wore the stola, which had short sleeves when the long-sleeved tunic was worn underneath and no sleeves when the tunic had short sleeves. The outdoor garment was the palla, which took different forms. It was sometimes worn like the toga, and often had an opening for the head and even a hood. The rich women wore veils and ornamented hairpins, diadems, ear-rings, bracelets, and rings on all fingers. Originally the favourite colour for the Roman dress was white, then scarlet, purply green, crocus yellow, pale mauve, and amethyst, checked materials and gold brocades came into favour. In spite of the imperial edict women and even men exposed themselves on all occasions covered only with transparent brightly coloured materials embroidered with gold and silver.

The types which evolved among others as stock characters in the Roman comedies written in the Greek spirit were the bullying father, the dissolute son, the cunning slave, the greedy procurer, the mercenary prostitute, the hungry toady, the bragging soldier, etc. For each of these there was a characteristic costume. The himation or chlamys, which showed the wearers to be Greeks, was generally a part of it. Those in distress appeared in careless attire, the slave in clothes of very short cut; the soldier wore the chlamys, and the toady a tight himation. All the actors in comedies wore low shoes called "soccus." Great importance appears to have been attached to colour in dress worn in comedies. Old men wore white, whereas youth, besides wearing white, decked itself in various colours. White also signified pleasure, red was a sign of wealth, dark hues portrayed poverty, procurers wore a gay-coloured himation, hetairæ yellow. The cheerful slave had a white costume as his permanent stage dress, from which arose the term "mimus albus." Thus he appears, for instance, on Pompeian wall-paintings in a long white tunic and white pointed cap or in a short white tunic, white chlamys, and green hat.

Frescoes depicting theatrical scenes, discovered in 1879 in a house in Pompeii, give one a good idea of the colours worn by actors at the time in which that little city flourished. The plays from which these scenes were taken seem to belong to the time of Ptolemaus Philadelphus, and depict both tragic and comic subjects.

The tragic actors wear the long-sleeved wide chiton which is familiar from pictures of Greek actors. A dignified old man in a tragic scene, for example, is clad in one of these robes of yellow, with a broad mauve hem decorated in yellow. Other tragic actors of more youthful appearance are in tight green chitons and cloaks, or yellow chitons and yellow and green chlamys, and a youth, probably intended for Achilles, has a mauve chiton and chlamys. An old man next to him, probably Priam, is shown in a yellow chiton and chlamys of the same

ROMAN TRAGIC ACTOR
Dress. Mask. Cothurnus.

hue. A boy in a tragic scene is in violet, a woman in the same scene wears a light-green chiton and cloak, and a young girl a long-sleeved chiton of a whitish green hue. An actress, who is meant to represent Medea, is in a light-green chiton with sleeves with a red girdle, but has no cloak.

Among the figures in comic scenes depicted in these frescoes are men wearing light-green chitons and yellow cloaks, short pale yellow and mauve chitons. A pedagogue wears a violet chiton and a yellow cloak, a boy a yellow chiton and cloak, a youth the same in white, a woman a chiton of pale green and a yellow cloak, and a prostitute a greenish-blue chiton.

In the time of the Cæsars, stripes and geometrical designs appeared on the material of which tragic costumes were made. The ivory statuette of a tragic actor of that period shows a blue chiton with perpendicular yellow stripes, while the sleeves have horizontal stripes of the same colour.

Plautus has given us in his comedy a complete picture of the dress of the "Miles Gloriosus," who appears in a short exomis which leaves the left breast bare. Over the left shoulder is slung a dark-brown cloak, and a slouch hat of the same colour is on the head with a flap over the brow. In the copies of Terence in various handwritings, which are preserved in the Vatican, Paris, Milan, and Leipzig, are to be found descriptions of scenes from this author's comedies giving vivid pictures of the appearance of the Roman comic actors during the final phase of the ancient theatre.

Besides Tragedy and Comedy, Pantomime and Mime also existed in the Roman theatre. The Pantomime was a sort of solo Ballet, a characteristic dance, which, to the accompaniment of song and musical instruments, presented either a comic or pathetic theme. It has been described by Apuleius and other Antique writers and, together with the Moorish dances of the Middle Ages known as Moresca, the Pantomime may be considered as one of the originators of the "classic"

Ballet. In the pantomime a single actor represented a series of male and female impersonations, changing masks and dresses. Pantomime dances had long been practised in Greece. They came from Greece to Etruria and thence to Rome. Two Greeks, Pylades of Cilicia and Bathyllus of Alexandria were famous at this time for pantomime dances. The subjects chosen were from Greek Mythology, such as the stories of Venus, Helen and Paris, Castor and Pollux, and various gods, goddesses, demi-gods, and heroes. At first only men danced in pantomime, and it was not until the time of the late Cæsars that women took part in them. As men had danced in the rôles of women, so women now took men's parts, and did not hesitate to appear as famous heroes, for we read that under Justinian a girl dancer appeared as Hector. This pantomime dancing had great sensual allure, and it is only natural, therefore, that considerable importance was attached to the costume. The most costly transparent materials from the East were sometimes worn. This transparent stuff, when worn, for instance, as a tunic reaching to the feet, intended apparently to cover the body and yet concealing nothing, probably had a far greater effect on the sensual emotions of the onlookers than if, as Apuleius relates, Venus appeared in a pantomime quite naked, or, according to Valerius Maximus, the dancers in the *Florealia* stripped themselves and danced naked. Some investigators, however, state that this "undressing" should only be taken to mean that the male and female dancers removed their outer garments in order to appear in short, light underclothes, which allowed the forms and movements of the body to be visible. Such light sandals were worn that the dancers appeared to be bare-footed. Female dancers are depicted in Etruscan wall-paintings in light, transparent tunics, while their dressers, who of course did not appear on the stage, are fully clothed. It has been claimed that the pictures on Etruscan mirrors owe their origin to these pantomime dances, which were very popular among the Etruscans at the time in which mirrors were first introduced. All those characters and stories which have been mentioned by ancient writers as being characteristic of these pantomime dances (Bacchus and Ariadne, the Judgment of Paris, etc.) are to be found on these mirrors and emphasize the fact that the costume worn was exceedingly light. It is obvious that public performances in such scanty garb, and of a nature which worked entirely on the senses, did not fail to have an influence on the people engaged in them, and the women dancers in Rome were considered as prostitutes. The Emperor Caligula is said to have danced in Pantomime himself. This maniac liked to play the part of Venus, and at the end of his performance let his garments fall and appeared in a state of nature in the presence of his admirers.

The Roman Mimes were farces played without masks. Owing to their satirical and strongly obscene nature, they ousted under the Emperors serious Drama from the stage as a form of amusement of the upper classes and even of the populace. The two most celebrated writers of Mimes in the Latin tongue were Decimus Laberius and Publilius Syrus. Philistion, however, wrote Mimes in Greek for the Roman "upper ten thousand" (who alone understood Greek), and these soon became popular among the educated classes in the provinces. Women appeared in Mimes from their inauguration.

The costume peculiar to Mimes was a gay-coloured patchwork, called the *centunculus,* similar to the dress worn by Maccus of the Atellanæ and to that of the Italian Harlequin. Probably this costume, however, was only worn by the fool of the Mimes, Stupidus, who was always represented with shaven head and was the recipient of endless blows and resounding boxes on the ears. Certain documents indicate that the word "centunculus" became the name applied to Mime actors in general. On a tomb-painting at Corneto a Stupidus is portrayed wearing a short coat which is made of material divided into small squares, obviously the coloured patches which gave the garment its name of centunculus. On his head he wears a tall pointed cap, striped vertically, with a tassel at the top. The feet were encased in flat-soled, sock-like shoes, which allowed them to be perfectly flat on the ground, and hence the Mime players were also called *planipes*. This costume was completed by a square-cut short cloak known as the *ricinium*. From this garment the Mime players were also known as *riciniati*.

Different life-like Roman types appeared in Mimes such as soldiers, orators, shopkeepers, sausage-makers, innkeepers, masters and servants, love-sick women, and young people of all sorts. So that the subject of the scene might be intelligible to the onlookers, all these people must always have worn characteristic costumes on the stage. Even the honourable dress of the Roman citizen, the toga, was worn in Mime. Cyprian speaks of a deceived husband appearing on the stage in a toga.

The producers of Mimes provided the male performers in these shows with gigantic phalluses. The Mimes, it has been said, "pulled down gods and heroes from on high and provided them with phalloi."

Acting without masks, the introduction of female players, and the actors' appearance on the stage in the ordinary garb of citizens were three factors which encouraged vanity and rivalry among the players, and inevitably led to a display of luxury and magnificence in the matter of costume, which reached a great height in the time of the Cæsars. In the sixth century the dresses of women acting in Mimes were described as "glittering with gold and pearls."

Religion of every sort was very hostile to Mimes, as they not only poked fun at the gods of Olympus, but also parodied the Mysteries of the early Christians and their religious ceremonies. Religious-minded people have left some vivid accounts of the wastefulness and display of the Mime players. According to St. Chrysostom, the female players not only appeared with bare heads, but curled their hair elaborately, painted their faces, and adorned themselves with such an amount of gold, silver, and pearls and wore such seductive clothing that he warned Christian wives not to wear cloth-of-gold "like actresses." The male performers also aroused St. Chrysostom's contempt and anger, and he speaks of young men appearing with waved hair and got up effeminately and affecting women's charms.

The mask was unknown in the Roman tragedy and comedy until the time of Pacuvius, before which actors had painted their faces and worn wigs. Only those noble young Roman citizens who appeared in the Atellanæ possessed the right to wear masks (or persona larva) so that they might remain unrecognized. The actor Roscius seems to have been the first to act in a mask. Cicero, in the year 55 B.C., wrote that everyone could still remember acting without masks. The introduction of masks in Rome must have taken place about 100 B.C. The example of Roscius succeeded in establishing the wearing of masks in the Roman theatre in spite of the hostility of the older generation. As neither the Roman actors nor spectators wished to be deprived of the play of features, the masks were made with such large openings for the eyes and mouth that these remained clearly visible. Tragic masks worn on the Roman stage were made in the Greek style. Some writers praise the manner in which the dæmonic rage of Medea, the virility of Hercules, and the dejection of Ajax were vividly expressed in the features of the masks worn. When the Emperor Nero appeared in tragedies in the rôles of gods or heroes he wore masks depicting his own features, but on the occasions of his playing goddesses he would appear in masks representing the features of the women he loved. The masks worn in Comedy seem to have corresponded to those used in Greece. They comprised a selection of stock types of panders, soldiers, peasants, youths, prostitutes, and others. The example set by playing Mime without masks resulted in their being abandoned in Comedy also. According to one Roman writer of the middle of the fourth century B.C., Terence's *Andria* was being played again in his time without masks and with women playing the female parts.

With the downfall of the Roman Empire and the decadence of the ancient civilization the regular public theatre disappeared in Europe, and the theatrical art was carried on only by jesters and vagabond players in the market-places, the inns, and the fairs. Much later, however, the theatrical spirit innate in mankind took the form of the regular public theatre again in liturgical dramatic fragments and in Church Mystery Plays.

CHAPTER IV

THE MIRACLE PLAYS AND MORALITIES

THE earliest regular theatrical performances in Western and Central Europe and those parts of Eastern Europe where the people professed the Roman Catholic religion after Greek and Roman times were the representations of the Mystery and Miracle plays produced in churches.

Even in Russia, where they appeared much later than the rest of Europe, although theatrical performances and all attempts at masquerading were anathema to the Greek Orthodox Church, little "interludes" were added to certain ceremonies of that "righteous and glorious" Church to attract believers. These were the so-called "Washing of the Feet," "The Procession on the Donkey," and "The Stew of the Oven." With the exception of parts of "the Wicked Chaldeans" in the last interlude, which were considered unsuitable and beneath the dignity of the clergy, and were played in the ordinary peasant dress of the period by professional strolling vagabond jesters called "Skomorokhs," all the rôles were performed by the priests and deacons in their usual sacerdotal robes. These were more or less the same as those we see on bishops, priests, deacons, and sub-deacons (psalomstchik) of the Russian Church of our own day.

As the masses belonging to the Roman Catholic confession could neither read the Bible in Latin nor understand the Latin church service, a theatrical representation was found to be a most suitable and attractive means of instilling Holy Writ and Church Legend into the people. The legends in particular were adapted by the clergy at festivals to celebrate the day of the saint to whom their church happened to be dedicated. The saint's day was an occasion on which people flocked in from the neighbouring country, and it was hoped, by pageants and impressive representations of the miracles which the saint had wrought and of the sufferings he had undergone, that both the saint and the church might be rewarded by some special benefit from on high. The "Mysteries" in their infancy were more epic than dramatic in character, and were written in Latin, the lines being delivered in a kind of minor sing-song and hammered *recitativo*. This method of speaking lines was subsequently used by most tragic actors of the secular theatre until about the end of the eighteenth century. "Le système de déclamation"—wrote Talma— "était alors une psalmodie de triste mélodie, qui datait de la naissance du théâtre." The responses by the congregation were made in the vernacular, which gradually superseded the Latin altogether. After the introduction of the historical element into the religious service the next step was to bring dogma into these presentations, since it was clear that the dogmas of the church could not be made more plain to the people than by a theatrical representation of a "miracle" or some other supernatural event. The name "Miracle play," which was used at an early date, and appears to have ousted the name "Mystery," proves what a prominent feature miracles played in the Church performances.

The earliest Mystery and Miracle plays were performed within the precincts of the churches themselves, and were acted by the priests, not, however, in the manner in which we understand that word, but rather suggested, and the costumes worn were merely the usual Roman Catholic ecclesiastical garments.

The Catholic ecclesiastical vestments originally consisted of a long white linen Roman tunica talaris, known as the *alba,* with long sleeves and cuffs. Over the alba a flat belt was fastened. After the ninth century the ecclesiastical costume became more elaborate, and the alba was decorated with embroidery and precious stones down the front seam; it was often of silk, and the belt was enriched. Over the alba was the *stola*—a long narrow band, frequently adorned with crosses. It was placed round the neck, crossed on the chest, and held under the belt, and its edges were sometimes decorated with embroidery and bells. The garment worn by the priests for celebrating Mass had been the *casula* (chasuble). This was a decorative costume in the shape of a bell with an opening for the head. The *dalmatic*—a broad tunic with wide square sleeves—came into use in the eleventh century, and was put on over the alba. From the end of the twelfth century a semicircular cloak of heavy material called a *pluviale* was also in use. An elongated kerchief, known as an *amictus* or *superhumerale,* was placed round the neck. The head-dress was the pointed cap and the mitre or tiara.

The priests were in these costumes when they played the parts of heavenly characters and saints in the church plays. In some rôles they carried various objects suggestive of the characters they were playing. The parts of angels were taken by priests and choir-boys dressed in albas, or albas and dalmatics, with palm leaves and other emblems in their hands, sometimes carrying wings on their backs, sometimes not.

Female characters were, of course, acted by priests, and to indicate that they represented women, they merely put the amictus over their heads and left the rest to the imagination of the public. When the pluviale came into fashion it was draped in the manner of a woman's cloak.

We find in the MS. of one of the first Easter Resurrection plays a direction which shows that details from "worldly" costumes were used by ecclesiastical performers, and that they wore false beards. Thus it says in this MS. that Christ appears twice in different costumes, the first time in the ordinary dress of a "gardener," and the second in an ecclesiastical white dalmatic with a crown on the head, and a flag with a cross upon it, as a sign of the sufferings He had undergone, in the right hand and an Evangelium in the left. In that part of the MS. dealing with the appearance of Christ on the way to Emmaus we read: "Two ecclesiastics enter as pilgrims dressed in cloaks (pluviale) over albas, with staffs and sacks in their hands. They must wear *hats* and *beards*. Christ, whom they meet, must wear an alba and an amictus, be barefooted, and carry a cross on the left shoulder. The woman who has to act in this scene must be played by an ecclesiastic in a dalmatic with an amictus placed over the head, as worn by women." At the appearance of Christ to the apostle Thomas we read that the doubting Thomas wore a silk tunic, an appropriate non-clerical hat, and had a staff in his hand.

The ecclesiastical Christmas plays dealing with the birth of Christ were more complicated than those concerned with the Resurrection. They had many more characters, and much more elaborate plots, and therefore required more variety and more realism in the matter of costumes, make-up, and properties. In the *Play of the Prophets*—one of the Nativity performances and very popular in France—various characters of the Old and New Testaments appeared as defenders of the Christian faith. Of these, Moses was dressed in an alba, had horns on his head, wore a long beard, and held the ten commandments in one hand and a rod in the other. Daniel appeared as a young man in a green tunic with a spear in his hand; Balaam, with spurs, rode the famous ass; Nebuchadnezzar, whose guards were in armour, had decorations suitable to the dignity of a king and held a statuette of an idol in his hand. In *The Play of the Three Kings,* which originated in the eleventh century in France, the three kings appeared in silk vestments and golden crowns, and carried precious vessels in their hands.

By degrees secular comic elements to attract the public were introduced into the church plays, "improprieties" of various kinds crept in, and from an ecclesiastical point of view it became desirable for the Popes and Church Councils to forbid the priests taking part in the religious plays, and parish clerks, ministrants, lay-brothers, and strolling players took their places. Furthermore, the priests were no longer numerous enough for the ever-increasing crowd of characters introduced into the plays, and for this reason also non-ecclesiastics, amateurs, and professional players were called upon to participate. The more the religious plays developed as dramas, the more inevitable it became to admit the secular element, and to depart, in spirit as well as in fact, from the place of their origin. In 1210 Pope Innocent III forbade the plays being given in churches, and prohibited the wearing of masks by secular players, so that the plays were perforce held in the churchyards. But they were not allowed to remain long even there, and soon churchyards were also forbidden ground. After the thirteenth century dramatic performances were gradually thrust on to the streets and market-places, where they eventually became completely secularized, both as regards performers and themes.

In England, Mystery plays—which were introduced from France shortly after the Conquest—fell into the hands of the laity earlier than elsewhere; at least, so it would seem, as the oldest Mystery and Miracle plays preserved in this country are distinctly in the popular style and not of early ecclesiastical character. Perhaps the chief reason for the laity participating in these performances was the introduction of the feast of Corpus Christi by Popes Urban IV (1264) and Clement V (1311). As this festival fell in the most favourable season of the year—on the first Thursday after Trinity, i.e. twelve days after Whit-Sunday—it soon became a big national holiday which probably came to include the ancient "pagan" merry-makings of May Day and Whitsuntide.

> "At Pentecost,
> When all our pageants of delight were play'd,
> Our youth got me to play the woman's part. . . ."

After leaving the church and its precincts, the purpose of religious plays was to present the life and sufferings of Christ, and from the thirteenth century, i.e. for three hundred years, this remained their object, and they were known as Passion plays.

The secular comic element already began to creep into church performances in the eleventh century. For instance, to amuse the public, the priests introduced the character of a vendor into the scene of the three Marys on the way to Christ's grave, from whom they had to buy the salves. The vendor was, of course, dressed in the ordinary townsman's costume of the period. As it was very often necessary to have numerous servants and peasants in these plays, and as such parts were beneath the dignity of the priests and other ecclesiastics, amateurs and strolling professional players were engaged for them, who, naturally, made the most of their parts and were a great success with the audience. The priests, noting this, and eager to have a "full house" at any price—just like modern theatrical managers— began to give important rôles to secular players, who usually turned them into comedy. It was thus, for instance, that Joseph, the husband of Mary, very soon became a sot and miser, and was shown on the way to Egypt quarrelling with the innkeeper (another comic character), and even having "rows" with the Holy Mother herself. In the Towneley Mystery play, *The Murder of Abel,* the part of Cain was acted by a secular player with a Yorkshire accent, much to the amusement of the audience. In the fourteenth century Caspar, the youngest of the kings in *The Three Kings,* began to be played as a black man (often in a mask), which made him appear very comic indeed to the unsophisticated spectators. In order to please the public taste that part gradually came to be acted in a very crude, farcical way. Herod was another who very quickly became a funny character, and the small comic parts of the devils, who were introduced into religious plays at the end of the eleventh century and played by lay performers, very soon developed into the most important rôles in the plays. The demand for comic relief was so great that even God the Father himself, dressed in a richly decorated casula with a sceptre in his hand and a mitre on the head, indulged in such jokes as would never pass the Lord Chamberlain's office nowadays.

When no longer produced by the churches the plays were taken over by the Guilds, and in the towns where these were particularly flourishing, the plays attained a high standard of production. Not only did the day of the performance draw great crowds from all parts, but it was one on which a vast amount of business was transacted, and it was thus to the interest of the Guilds to attract as many people as possible. Each Guild possessed its own Miracle plays, or rather its series or succession of plays, and was responsible for the manner in which the performances were staged and acted. In England the tanners of Chester used to play *The Fall of Lucifer,* the drapers *The Creation and Fall and Death of Abel,* and the water-carriers *The Story of Noah's Flood.*

Considerable sums of money were spent in erecting and decorating the scaffolding or stage, the costumes, etc., and the performers, who had beforehand to give proof of their skill, were paid according to the length of their parts and the amount of work they had to do and not according to their talents. God the Father received 2*s.*, the Devil and Judas 1*s.* 6*d.*, while Herod, on account of the exhausting nature of the part, with "obbligato" storms of rage, got 3*s.* 4*d.*

The different scenes of the play's action (episodes) were set alongside each other on the same public place or square.

"Imaginez sur la Grand'Place des tréteaux dressés le long des maisons opposées à l'Hôtel de Ville. Des décors—toiles peintes montées sur châssis—et des *practicables* s'y sont dressés, bariolés de vermillon et de cendre d'azur. Il n'y en eut pas moins de quinze représentant les *lieux* par lesquels doit passer l'action. Les deux maîtresses pièces en sont aux deux extrémités de la scène: le *Paradis,* à gauche du spectateur et à droite de Dieu, et l'*Enfer.* Au Paradis sur un trône élevé, Dieu en manteau de pourpre bordé de martre, comme dans le retable de l'Agneau à Saint Bavon de Gand, entouré d'anges exhalant harmonieusement sa louange. L'Enfer est une forteresse hérissée de canons, dont les bordées de feu accueilleront

Jésus, quand il viendra délivrer les Pères des Limbes. Lucifer en-chaîné y règne sur ses diables hideux, qui ne sortent que par l'horrible et grimaçante Gueule d'Enfer, laquelle vomit les cris des damnés roués, ébouillantés, torturés.

"La représentation, préparée plus de six mois à l'avance, dura huit jours, matinée et après-midi, du 4 au 11 Juillet, et eut un prodigieux succès, malgré l'inexpérience des acteurs, clercs, bourgeois et artisans. S'ils n'ont pas la science, ils ont la conviction et se pénètrent si bien de leur rôle qu'ils en gardent longtemps le nom et l'attitude. *La com-pagnie infernale* boit à *la Clef,* celle de Dieu *au Cerf.* On trouve même dans les *Compte des Dépenses,* pour le Mystère de la Passion joué a Mons en 1501, cette mention singulière: '*A Dieu le père, un pot de vin, . . . cinq sous!*' C'était là sa seule récompense pour avoir travaillé à la gloire de son modèle."

In England the Miracle plays, as well as the Moralities, to which we will come later in this chapter, were of two kinds, stationary and processional. The stationary variety were given on a series of plat-forms, fixed or movable, and arranged so as to suit the play. The processional productions were also staged on platforms, but on wheels, which moved in processions (pageants) through the town, each plat-form stopping at the place chosen for the performance of that par-ticular scene. The festivities and merry-making of knights and squires frequently joined these processions of the Guilds' shows.

David Rogers writes in his Breviary of the City of Chester in 1609: "The maner of these playes were every company had his pagiant, which pagiante weare a high scafold with 2 rowmes, a higher and a lower upon 4 wheels. In the lower they apparelled them-selves, and in the higher rowme they played, beinge all open on tope, that all beholders might heare and see them. The places where they played them was in every streete. They began first at the Abay gates, and when the first pagiante was played, it was wheeled to the highe crosse before the Mayor, and so to every streete, and soe every

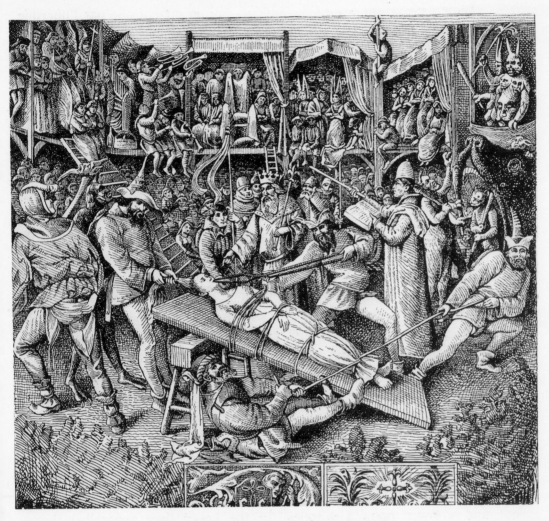

THE MYSTERY OF ST. APOLLONIA
15th century

streete had a pagiante playing before them at one time, till all the pagiantes for the day appointed weare played, and when one pagiant was neere ended, word was brought from streete to streete, that soe they might come in place thereof, exceedinge orderly, and all the streetes have their pagiants afore them all at one time playeinge together, to see which playes was great resorte; and also scafolds and stages made in the streetes in those places where they determined to play theire pagiantes."

Amongst the processions (pageants) the most famous were those of *Christ's entry into Jerusalem, Christ's going to Pilate, The Angels and the Shepherds,* and *The Three Kings,* who rode on horseback, surrounded by a big and richly dressed suite. We frequently find scenes from the processions of *The Three Kings* in the pictures of Italian Renaissance artists.

The dresses at first worn by the higher celestial and saintly personages in the Miracles performed without the precincts of the churches were borrowed from the church. The "worldly" characters wore the ordinary dress of the time or those of the vagabond players —as the lay performers had done when acting in the churches—which they usually had to supply at their own expense. Although we notice in the performances of the Miracles the desire to endow the shows with a certain local colour by means of costumes, there was never even an attempt to make them historically correct. Until the end of the fifteenth century people had no idea that the inhabitants of the ancient world did not dress as they did, nor did it occur to them that God and the saints could look in any way different from the priests. By the sixteenth century all the principal parts in religious plays had traditional costumes, so that there were often no other directions given in the MSS. than, for instance, "habitus patriarchalis," "prophetalis," or "apostolicus," or "the King and his suite are dressed in the usual way."

The characteristic and symbolic touches to the ecclesiastics' vestments and the "modern" dresses of the lay performers were supplied by means of details and colour. Particular attention was paid to the symbolic touches. For instance, in the *The Last Judgment* at the Coventry pageant the "Saved Souls" wore long *white* tunics and the "Damned Souls" *black*. In a continental Passion play Christ appeared first in a purple ecclesiastical dress and after the resurrection in bright red. The Mother of God usually wore a light-blue cloak in her earlier years, but when more aged and as a spectator at her Son's martyrdom on the Cross she was clad in dark blue or even black. At her death she was usually in white. Sometimes she had a crown on her head. Judges wore yellow, the colour of cunning. It was probably towards the fifteenth century that wings were definitely added to the angels, who before then frequently appeared not only in white but also in gold and red dalmatics. In the Coventry pageant the angels wore a species of cothurnus or short stilts to appear more impressive. The only actors in the Miracles who wore realistic "character" costumes were the devils. They were usually got up to look like snakes *sub specie virginis*, i.e. with the faces of virgins, or like dragons, bulls, dogs, and monsters. Their costumes were made of skins, with horns, tails, claws, wings, etc. The "virginal" and the various animals' faces were either masks, or the performers painted their faces and hands with the "innocent" whitewash or the "hellish" black. The masks covered either the face or the whole head. At the Coventry pageant the devils had head-masks. The dress worn by Satan himself in the same pageant— a tight-fitting garment of canvas, smeared with glue and horsehair— was sewn on to the performer. At Chester feathers were used instead of horsehair. Sometimes devils appeared in human form as hermits, varlets, comic doctors, kings, and even as old women. Female devils, who began to make their appearance on the stage at the beginning of the sixteenth century, were clad either in black "modern" women's dresses with green and red "trappings," or in fur skins, like the male devils, and had pendulant breasts with long nipples, from which spurted blood or fire. They wore terrifying masks and horsehair wigs, with or without horns. The female devils were, of course, played as a rule by men.

As the "worldly" costume grew more elaborate from the ninth century onwards, and began to be made of more and more expensive materials, the production of religious plays, especially from the fourteenth century, gradually became quite extravagant. The costumes of the Miracle plays, although remaining ecclesiastic or "modern" in form, gradually lost their severity when made of expensive materials, and began to be heavily decorated with fantastic details. These were intended to satisfy the growing taste for luxury, to supply local colour more vividly, and to give a symbolical significance to the costumes. In the production of a Mystery play about St. Barbara in France in 1493, even the devils were dressed in velvet, silk, and brocade. To satisfy the demand of the public for spectacular effects and intrigues, the performers of certain parts began to change their costumes during the performance. The devils were no exception to this innovation, and tormented their victims in different guises. Most of the money spent on the production of a religious pageant in France in 1503 went on the staging of Hell. Yet there were other productions in which the angels did not lag behind their wicked brethren in the matter of rich embellishment. After the end of the fourteenth century angels no longer appeared in simple albas or plain dalmatics, but in dalmatics of brocade, cloaks, casulas, and sometimes even in crowns. In Italy their enriched and coloured tunics often fell in folds from the belt and formed a kind of "buff" round their hips. Some of them wrote tight-fitting bodices, and the Archangel Michael is usually portrayed in armour. Italian angels frequently wore women's dresses and the everyday clothes of smart young men of the period, but with wings and shining discs at the back of the head to represent halos. Jews were usually distinguished by tall hats with the brims often cut into pointed teeth, and by their long coats.

An idea of the fantastic elements in the costumes of the religious plays of the later Middle Ages may be obtained from the paintings of such artists as Pesellino (the "stories" of "Cosmo and Damian" and "St. Nicholas" in Florence, and "Griseldis" in the Carrara Gallery at Bergamo), Taddeo Gaddi, Fra Angelico da Fiesole, Ambrogio Lorenzetti, Pollajuolo, Benozzo Gozzoli, Hans Baldung Grien, Konrad Witz, Hans Fries, N. M. Deutsch, Lucas Cranach, Lucas van Leyden, Rogier van der Weyden, Van Eyck, H. Memling, etc., and certain tapestries and illuminated MSS. and stained-glass windows. The statues round the tomb of the Emperor Maximilian in the Court Church at Innsbrück are also interesting as examples of the elaborately decorated costumes of the Miracle plays.

The hiring of lay performers and the pandering to the taste of the public when the plays no longer took place in the churches accounted for the introduction, not only of "worldly" luxury and the language of the market-place, but also of erotic and coarse naturalistic elements. We find directions in the earlier religious plays to the effect that Adam and Eve, Christ and various martyrs should appear nude. Yet this was by no means a general rule. At that time the nakedness of these characters was merely suggested, or they wore proper costumes. In documents relating to the later religious plays we discover that nakedness was represented in a much more naturalistic way than in earlier times. In *The Creation of the World*, Adam and Eve, who appeared before the fall "in Whytt lether," received afterwards from the Angel "garmentis of skyness." In the Chester pageant Christ on the Cross wore tights of white leather on which his wounds were painted. In a play produced in Dresden in 1480, Adam and Eve appeared in tights made of white linen. On the Continent Christ sometimes appeared naked, with his body painted white and a cloth round the loins. In a play produced in the

714 b INNSBRUCK, Hofkirche, Statuengr...

STATUES SURROUNDING THE TOMB OF
THE EMPEROR MAXIMILIAN

Hofkirche, Innsbrück

fourteenth century on the Alta Carraia bridge over the Arno at Florence, the "suffering souls," both men and women, appeared quite naked. The success of this production was so great that the bridge collapsed under the immense crowd of spectators. In the sixteenth century in England Adam and Eve appeared in garments which presented nakedness so realistically that a contemporary writer was shocked by their indecency. They amused the public in the first scene, he said, by talking about those parts of their bodies which they covered up with fig leaves in the following scene. The appearance of women in plays, however, until they really began to take part in theatrical productions in the seventeenth century, was exceptional. Erotic excitement was provided in these Mediæval shows by men made up as women. In the second half of the fifteenth century, to strengthen the sexual appeal of a show, women were sometimes allowed to take part, which they usually did by exhibiting their sexual charms. They were regarded, not as actresses, but merely as females or even whores. One of the first women, who played the title rôle in *The Mystery of Saint Katherine* in 1468, in Metz, was a girl thirteen years of age, but she did not remain long on the stage, as she married one of the spectators immediately after the show.

The extremes to which naturalism was carried in religious plays given outside the churches was, of course, due to the coarse taste of the times and the strong nerves of the public. In a crucifixion scene Christ had a pig's bladder filled with red liquid under his tights, which was pierced by the spear of the Roman soldier. When Judas hanged himself devils tore open his "belly" and "his bowels fell out," and "his soul," represented by a live bird or a black squirrel, was carried off by the servants of Hell. For this Judas had to carry a bag containing animals' bowels and a bird or squirrel under his clothes. It was customary for Christ to be slowly hoisted high up on to the cross by ropes, which greatly pleased the public, and even sometimes aroused laughter. The martyred saints, men and women (the latter represented by men, of course), were tortured in a most realistic way, for which scenes dummies were substituted for the actors.

From the Miracle plays sprang the Moralities and the St. George plays, the latter of which were influenced by the knights' tournaments. In England the plays about St. George and the dragon were always great favourites both with the populace and the Court, and were connected, like the Miracle and Morality plays, with processions. In these shows St. George wore knightly armour with helmet and spurs. The King's daughter appeared in modern dress, and the Dragon was made of iron and wood covered with velvet or other expensive material of suitable colours to imitate the dragon's skin and decorated with gold and silver. The drawings of the Florentine ironsmith Caparra show us one of these "prop" dragons.

The Morality plays were of more or less "worldly" character. The main interest of the Moralities lay in the original plots (often inspired by Mythology), in the allegory (although historical Moralities were in existence) in allegorical characters, and in the modern types. Impersonations of the virtues and vices, and above all the seven cardinal virtues and the seven deadly sins, together with Poverty, Age, the World, the Soul, Death, etc., were the chief rôles. In the Miracle plays certain allegorical personages had already been introduced and the public was accustomed to them. In *Tom Tylor and his Wife,* which was done in England in 1578, we find alongside Desire, Strife, Patience and Vice, the realistic figures of Tom Tylor, his wife, and his friend. In the Morality, *The Conflict of Conscience, contayninge the most lamentable Hystorye of the desperation of Frauncis Spera, who forsooke the trueth of God's Gospell for feare of the losse of life and worldly goodes,* which was written about 1570, there appear side by side with the impersonations of Conscience, Hypocrisy, Tyranny, and Avarice, four historical characters, namely, the Italian lawyer Francesco Spiera and his two sons and Cardinal Eusebius.

HECTOR AND AGAMEMNON
A 15th century representation of the Greek Heroes

The Moralities were usually staged on one single scaffold in a public place, a hall, or an inn yard. Some of these plays required stage-settings, others nothing but the bare scaffold and stage "props," and some were given without any accessories at all.

So that the allegory might not be tedious, nor the sententious speeches boring for the unsophisticated spectators, dances and songs, in addition to comic characters such as the Devil, Vice or Iniquity, were introduced into the Moralities, and the costumes were made as elaborate and rich as possible.

These were either "modern" or ecclesiastical with fantastic and allegoric touches added to them. For instance, the "Soul," acted by a girl, wore a white brocade dress decorated with precious stones, a black cloak, a wig and diadem. "Consolation" was dressed in blue, "Pieta" in white, and "Whoredom" was a very smart lady with a "wonderful" mask on her face. Venus had a dress and cloak of yellow silk painted with hearts, and silver wings on her back. Sometimes the allegorical characters had inscriptions on their headgear or other parts of their dress to make their meaning plainer to the audience, and not infrequently characters or supers who accompanied them carried boards on sticks or flags for the same purpose. In an English Morality play in 1528, the Apostles Peter and Paul appeared in silver wigs, white velvet coats, and red cloaks. Martin Luther in the same play wore a monk's dress of dark red and black silk and taffeta.

The Devil, who was provided with hoofs, tail, horns, and a bottle-nose, had been borrowed with all his costumes from the Miracle plays, whereas "Vice or Iniquity" was a new character, and, of course, indispensable if the qualities of "Virtue" were to be impressively exhibited. "Vice" was attired as a fool, and carried a long wooden switch or sword with which he incessantly belaboured the Devil, cut his claws, performed other pranks of a similar kind, and finally paid his account by being dragged by the Lord of Darkness to the infernal regions. "Vice" was made to utter moralizing speeches

and snatches of song similar to those found in abundance in Shakespeare at a later day. In the play, *The longer thou livest, the more
foole thou art,* the stage direction for the appearance of the chief
character, Moros, is given thus: "Here entreth Moros, counter-
faiting a vaine gesture and a foolish countenance, synging the foote
of many songes as fools were wont."

Painters like Giotto, in the Capella dell' Arena in Padua, Cosimo
Tura, Melozzo da Forli, Botticelli, Dürer, and others give us in their
paintings an idea of how allegorical characters were clothed in the
Moralities.

Allegorical costumes are still met with in the Renaissance plays.
In Kyd's *Jeronimo* we find Revenge. In *Titus Andronicus* Revenge
again appears with Rape and Murder by her side. The Second Part
of *King Henry IV* opens with a speech by Rumour, who is represented as being "full of tongues." Ben Jonson makes "Nobody" appear in trousers which begin at the neck, and in Hans Sachs's
Stultitia Stupidity wears a fool's cap.

Our modern productions of the Mediæval Morality plays, such as
Everyman staged by Max Reinhardt, at the Salzburg Festival, fall
very far beneath the original performances as regards the richness
and fantasy displayed by the costumes of the characters.

Sometimes the earlier Mediæval fashions were resorted to in the
Moralities as well as in the Miracle plays to give a suggestion of a
by no means too correct historical or local colour. As a rule the designers of costumes looked no farther back than one century. If, after
the fifteenth century, some of them did pry farther into the past, they
adapted the costumes of any age they fancied to the fashions of their
own day according to their own conception of that bygone time, and
to the passion for luxury of the actors and of the public. It is noticeable that throughout the history of theatrical costume every generation of actors, even the naturalists at the end of the nineteenth century, dressed themselves according to *their own* conception of a certain

THE MYSTERY OF THE PASSION
Rheims Cathedral   1500

epoch, and not according to the actual facts. And just as to-day, they were always ready to sacrifice the truth and beauty of simplicity for showiness and the over-elaboration of their fashionable costumes.

Various processions took place in connection with the perform-ances of the Moralities as they had with the Miracle plays. Proces-sions of Morality productions on wheeled scaffolds were known in Italy as "Trionfi." Many Renaissance artists took these as subjects for their paintings. Piero de Cosimo's "Triumph of Theseus and Ariadne," Botticelli's "The Triumph of Chastity," Sellaio's "The Triumph of Love" and "The Triumph of Chastity," are a few exam-ples. The Dances of Death, which were given in the streets, were processional interludes to the Moralities. The Moresca or Marusca dance, which was influenced by the Moors and Saracens, was also originally an interlude in the Morality plays, and only later became an independent entertainment. It was composed of pantomime, danc-ing, and fencing. Those who took part in the Moresca were dressed in fantastic "Moorish" costumes—combinations of "modern" fashion with Moorish style, with faces blackened in imitation of the Moors. In Germany the Moresca costumes were either "modern," with ex-aggerated, clownish details, or made of white tight-fitting material painted with flowers, leaves, stars, and various bright patterns, or of striped materials of different colours, sometimes half of the dress (horizontally or vertically) being of one colour and the other half another. In England the Moresca dances were known as Morris dances. For a Moresca danced in Mantua in 1542 the costumes were actually designed by the famous Giulio Romano. The Ballet, which originated from the Moresca, later became part of a new kind of performance known as Opera.

We have seen that comic relief in the Miracle plays was sup-plied by secular amateurs and professional players. The first were recruited by the ecclesiastical organizers of the shows from lovers of acting or from various amateur companies, strolling players who performed at the fairs, in the streets, public places and inns of towns and villages before an unsophisticated populace.

The performances given by the Mediæval professional vagabond actors and amateurs were distinctly anti-religious, and followed the traditions of the Atellanæ and Mime of Antiquity. These shows of pagan origin developed quite independently of the influence of the moral doctrines of the Christian Church, and were farcical and satirical in nature. Their satire was aimed against contemporary customs, manners, and persons, and the monologues and dialogues were usually subsidiary to matter which was purely entertaining for the masses, such as dances, songs, acrobatic feats, and clowning.

Very often shows given at the fairs were merely "stunts" for the sale of merchandise in the booths, or a means by which quacks, barbers, or charlatans might attract trusting clients. Sometimes tradesmen or "doctors" used themselves to perform in front of their booths or even on the pavements, and were occasionally assisted in this by members of their families. Not infrequently they hired assistants, who were either recruited from vagabond players or were ordinary town or village folk.

The costumes worn by these players who assisted trade, as well as by those amateurs and strolling players who produced satirical or clownish farces, were the same in cut and shape as those worn by the contemporary townsfolk and villagers. To add humour to the performances different comic details were added to the dresses— they were made too big or too small, or padded in grotesque fashion.

It was to masquerading processions arranged by villagers and townspeople during the Christmas and Shrove-tide holidays, together with performances of gossipy scenes from their everyday lives, that the so-called Shrove-tide plays owed their origin. As early as 1327 the Bishop of Pamiers in France forbade the performance of a Shrove-tide play called *Le Jeu des Cent Drutz,* which had as subject a "revue"

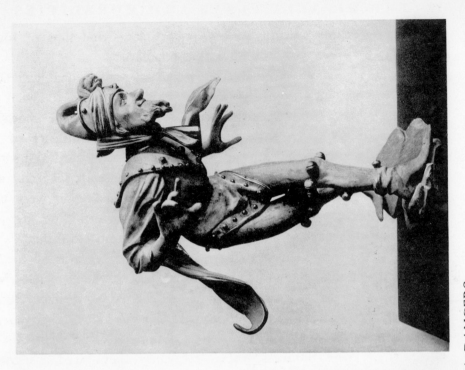

MORESCA DANCERS
Erasmus Grasser
City Hall, Munich   About 1480

of the events of the town, and in which young men "indecently" dressed up as women.

In the French *Sotties,* which also grew out of the Shrove-tide mummeries, different fools or jesters appeared, who, by their costumes and acting, poked fun at such respectable and permanent institutions as Universities, the Church, the Army, the Law, and Commerce. In one such *Sottie* the "Sot dissolu" appears dressed as a priest, the "Sot glorieux" dressed as a soldier, the "Sot corrompu" as a Judge, and the "Sot trompeur" as a tradesman. The character of the "Church" was represented in a play of this sort by a person arrayed as the Pope, but on being disrobed during the show the "Mother of all fools" was discovered hiding beneath his gorgeous apparel. The famous amateur company of actors, the "Clercs de la Basoche," incurred the anger of the authorities for daring to appear in masks representing faces of well-known people.

It is only very seldom that we hear of a dress of an earlier period being worn in these folk-shows or of a fantastic costume. All the costumes were contemporary, yet the satirical tendencies of the folk-shows and the attempt to make the contemporary dress of the comic characters appear humorous by making it, together with the figure of the wearer, grotesque and out of proportion resulted in the Middle Ages in the fantastic costume of the Fool or clown.

The use of masks representing animals, which had been the outstanding attributes of comic characters amongst vagabond players, began to die out about the year 1000. At the end of the fifteenth century, the pointed cap, which was worn by men and women in the fourteenth century, became a characteristic part of the Fool's costume. This cap, attached to a wide collar, covered the whole head, and left only the face visible. Donkey's ears, a sign of stupidity, were fixed to it, and bells were sewn on the points of the ears and sometimes on the seams. These bells were a relic of the ornaments on the dress of people of fashion in the thirteenth and fourteenth centuries. Some

Fools of the fifteenth century borrowed the cock's-comb for the top of the cap from the antique Atellanæ. Not infrequently, in place of the cock's-comb, fool's caps were trimmed with feathers. The cap was worn with any costume of any colour, preferably, of course, of a bright hue. Court Fools in the fifteenth century used to wear this cap with their livery uniform, from which subsequently sprang the multi-coloured costume of the jester, which had the front one colour and the back another, one leg blue and the other red, etc. The Mediæval custom of giving comic characters deformed bodies expressed itself in the costume of the Fool by adding a hump on the back and a protruding belly. These "funny" particularities were retained later on in some of the costumes of Capitanos in the *Commedia dell' Arte,* in those of the English Mr. Punch, of the German Hanswurst, and of the French Polichinelle.

CHAPTER V

IN THE TIME OF SHAKESPEARE

IN the sixteenth century, at the height of the Renaissance, when, through the spread of knowledge concerning the Antique world and the teaching of the Humanists, it was possible to attempt to understand real life without hindrance from clerical obscurantism, the secular drama came to life again, and the theatre began more and more to be the domain of professional secular playwrights and actors. The Morality and Mystery plays had for the most part fallen into the hands of secular players, and began to give way, not only to the newly revived Antique plays and imitation classic tragedy and comedy (*Commedia erudita*), but to original regular drama and comedy.

Literary plays had already been written, such as, for instance, the short dramas of the nun Roswitha in the tenth century, *Le Jeu de Saint Nicolas* by Jean Bodel in the thirteenth century, *Le Jeu de la Feuillée,* the first comic opera by Adam the hunchback, called De la Hale, and the pastorale *Robin et Marion;* but until the Renaissance these remained unique.

The great English Elizabethan plays owed their spectacular and aristocratic characters and their poetical polish to Antiquity and the Italian Renaissance, but their crude and bloody melodramatic realism in tragic moments, and the so-called "low" comic effects, to the English Mediæval popular shows and to the Moralities.

The influence of the Italian Renaissance dramatists upon Shakespeare (Ariosto, for example) is recognized, although it is the influence of the English national popular element which makes his plays human and actable, not the beauty of their language nor their frequently aristocratic subjects. These influences were reflected by the way in which his plays were acted and dressed.

73

Although the players of dramatic parts in the Elizabethan theatre still delivered their lines in the musical manner customary in the Moralities, they no longer used the chanting of Mediæval times, but a kind of realistic *declamation*. Although it seems almost incredible when one considers the modern English actor, yet there are reasons to believe that this was, furthermore, both passionate and clangorous in nature. There was, of course, no question of realism of speech as understood on the English stage of to-day and in the sense in which some of our modern actors try to act Shakespeare. Not only would under-emphasis and weak "restrained" gestures not have been tolerated in the English theatre of the sixteenth and seventeenth centuries, but even what is now accepted on the stage as "a natural way" of speaking would have been denounced as dull. The comic parts were acted in the Elizabethan theatre in a more or less realistic yet grotesque style, and the lines delivered were more staccato than those of the dramatic rôles.

As the people of those days thought that "modern" dress would make the productions seem more familiar and realistic to the audiences, in Shakespeare's time and until the end of the eighteenth century actors usually played any parts other than those they wanted to emphasize as foreign or Greek or Roman in the English dress of the time in which the plays were produced or in the dresses of a just by-gone age. When ancient Greeks or Romans had to appear, there would be a sort of attempt to dress the parts in something merely suggestive of Antique garb. For foreigners, anglicized outlandish dresses were used, and genuine historical costumes were sometimes worn. When Thomas Legge's *Richard the Third* was produced at a Cambridge college, the historical costumes preserved in the Tower were lent to the company.

The simplicity, plainness, and even poverty of scenic effects were some of the most characteristic features of the Elizabethan productions. But this environment did not affect the costumes of actors, which

—with the exception of the dresses of those actors who played characters belonging to the lower and poorer classes—were even more luxurious and extravagant than those of well-dressed people in real life during the reigns of Queen Elizabeth and James I.

"The fantastical folly of our nation," wrote William Harrison, in his *Description of England* (1587), "is such that no form of apparel liketh us longer than the first garment is in the wearing, if it continue so long, and be not laid aside to receive some other trinket newly devised by the fickle-headed tailors, who covet to have several tricks in cutting, thereby to draw fond customers to more expense of money. For my part, I can tell better how to inveigh against this enormity than describe any certainty of our attire; sithence such is our mutability, that to-day there is none to the Spanish guise, to-morrow the French toys are most fine and delectable, ere long no such apparel as that which is after the high Almain fashion, by and by the Turkish manner is generally best liked of, otherwise the Morisco gowns, the Barbarian fleeces, the mandilion worn to Colleyweston ward, and the short French breeches make a comely vesture that, except it were a dog in a doublet, you shall not see any so disguised as are my countrymen of England. And as these fashions are diverse, so likewise it is a world to see the costliness and the curiosity, the excess and the vanity, the pomp and the bravery, the change and the variety, and finally the fickleness and the folly, that is in all degrees, insomuch that nothing is more constant in England than inconstancy of attire. Oh, how much cost is bestowed nowadays upon our bodies, and how little upon our souls! How many suits of apparel hath the one, and how little furniture hath the other! How long time is asked in decking up the first, and how little space left wherein to feed the latter! How curious, how nice also, are a number of men and women, and how hardly can the tailor please them in making it fit for their bodies! How many times must it be sent back again to him that made it! What chafing, what fretting, what reproachful language, doth the poor workman bear away! And many times when he doth nothing to it at all, yet when it is brought home again it is very fit and handsome. Then must we put it on, then must the long seams of our hose be set by a plumb-line, then we puff, then we blow, and finally sweat till we drop, that our clothes may stand well upon us. I will say nothing of our heads, which sometimes are polled, sometimes curled, or suffered to grow at length like woman's locks, many times cut off, above or under the ears, round as by a wooden dish. Neither will I meddle with our variety of beards, of which some are shaven from the chin like those of Turks, not a few cut short like to the beard of Marquess Otto, some made round like a rubbing-brush, others with a piqué de vant (O! fine fashion), or now and then suffered to grow long, the barbers being grown to be so cunning in this behalf as the tailors. And therefore if a man have a lean and straight face, a Marquess Otto's cut will make it broad and large; if it be platter-like, a long slender beard will make it seem the narrower; if he be weasel-beaked, then much hair left on the cheeks will make the owner look big like a bowdled hen, and so grim as a goose, if Cornelis of Chelmsford say true. Many old men do wear no beards at all. Some lusty courtiers also and gentlemen of courage do wear either rings of gold, stones, or pearl in their ears, whereby they imagine the workmanship of God not to be a little amended. But herein they rather disgrace than adorn their persons, as by their niceness in apparel, for which I say most nations do not unjustly deride us, as also for that we do seem to imitate all nations round about us, wherein we be like to the polypus or chameleon; and thereunto bestow most cost upon our arses, and much more than upon all the rest of our bodies, as women do likewise upon their heads and shoulders.

"In women also, it is most to be lamented, that they do now far exceed the lightness of our men (who nevertheless are transformed from the cap even to the very shoe), and such staring attire, as in time past was supposed meet for none but light housewives only, is now

HENRY IRVING AS KING LEAR
The Enthoven Collection

become a habit for chaste and sober matrons. What should I say of their doublets with pendant codpieces on the breast, full of jags and cuts, and sleeves of sundry colours? Their galligaskins to bear out their bums and make their attire to fit plum round (as they term it) about them. Their farthingales, and diversely coloured nether stock of silk, jersey, and such like, whereby their bodies are rather deformed than commended?"

"The women in London," wrote the Duke Frederick of Würtemberg after his visit to England in 1592, "go dressed out in exceedingly fine clothes, and give all their attention to their ruffs and stuffs, to such a degree indeed, that many a one does not hesitate to wear velvet in the streets, which is common with them, whilst at home perhaps they have not a piece of dry bread."

"Ever since Evah was tempted," exclaimed indignantly the Puritan, Thomas Nashe, in his *Christs Teares over Jerusalem* (1593), "and the serpent prevailed with her, women have took upon them both the person of the tempted and the tempter. They tempt to be tempted, and not one of them, except she be tempted, but thinks herself contemptible. Unto the greatness of their great-grandmother Evah they seek to aspire, in being tempted and tempting. If not to tempt and be thought worthy to be tempted, why dye they and diet their faces with so many drugs as they do, as it were to correct God's workmanship, and reprove Him as a bungler, and one that is not His craftsmaster? Why ensparkle they their eyes with spiritualized distillations? Why tip they their tongues with aurum potabile? Why fill they age's frets with fresh colours?

"Their heads, with their top and top-gallant lawn baby-caps, and snow-resembled silver curlings, they make a plain puppet stage of. Their breasts they embusk up on high, and their round roseate buds immodestly lay forth, to shew at their hands there is fruit to be hoped. In their curious-antic-woven garments, they imitate and mock the worms and adders that must eat them. They shew the swellings of their mind, in the swellings and plumpings out of their apparel. Gorgeous ladies of the court, never was I admitted so near any of you, as to see how you torture poor old Time with sponging, pinning, and pouncing; but they say his sickle you have burst in twain, to make of your periwigs more elevated arches.

"It is not your pinches, your purls, your flowery jaggings, superfluous interlacings, and puffings up, that can any way offend God, but the puffing up of your souls, which therein you express. For as the biting of a bullet is not that which poisons the bullet, but the lying of the gunpowder in the dint of the biting: so it is not the wearing of costly burnished apparel that shall be objected unto you for sin, but the pride of your hearts, which (like the moth) lies closely shrouded amongst the threads of that apparel. Nothing else is garish apparel but pride's ulcer broken forth. How will you attire yourselves, what gown, what head-tire will you put on, when you shall live in hell amongst hags and devils?

"As many jags, blisters and scars shall toads, cankers and serpents make on your pure skins in the grave, as now you have cuts, jags or raisings, upon your garments. In the marrow of your bones snakes shall breed. Your morn-like crystal countenances shall be netted over and (masquer-like) caul-visarded with crawling venomous worms. Your orient teeth toads shall steal into their heads for pearl; of the jelly of your decayed eyes shall they engender them young. In their hollow caves (their transplendent juice so pollutionately employed), shelly snails shall keep house.

"Oh, female pride, this is but the dalliance of thy doom, but the intermissive recreation of thy torments. The greatness of thy pains I want portentous words to portray. Whereinsoever thou hast took extreme delight and glory, therein shalt thou be plagued with extreme and despiteous malady. For thy flaring frounced periwigs low dangled down with love-locks, shalt thou have thy head side dangled down with more snakes than ever it had hairs. In the mould of thy brain shall they clasp their mouths, and gnawing through every part of thy skull, ensnarl their teeth amongst thy brains, as an angler ensnarleth his hook amongst weeds.

"For thy rich borders, shalt thou have a number of discoloured scorpions rolled up together, and cockatrices that kill with their very sight shall continually stand spurting fiery poison in thine eyes. In the hollow cave of thy mouth, basilisks shall keep house, and supply thy talk with hissing when thou strivest to speak. At thy breasts (as at Cleopatra's), aspices shall be put out to nurse. For thy carcanets of pearl, shalt thou have carcanets of spiders, or the green venomous flies cantharides."

"Overlashing in apparel" on the Elizabethan stage was "so common a fault that the very hirelings of some of the players, which stand at reversion of six shillings by the week, jet it under gentlemen's noses in suits of silk, exercising themselves to prating on the stage, and common scoffing when they come abroad, where they look askance over the shoulder at every man, of whom the Sunday before they begged an alms."

Large and even extravagant sums were spent on elaborate stage dresses. It may be mentioned, for instance, that £4 14s. was given for a trunk-hose, and £16, and even as much as £20 10s. for a velvet cloak, and we should not forget that money possessed about five or six times the value then that it does now.

There appears to have been no attempt to illustrate the plays of Shakespeare and to reproduce the costumes worn by the actors in his plays until the beginning of the eighteenth century. The first illustrated issue of his plays was published in 1709 by Jacob Tonson, the famous bookseller, the editor of which was Nicholas Rowe, the poet-laureate of George I, and one of the most successful dramatists of Queen Anne's reign. The illustrations are, as Charles Lamb said, "execrably bad," but characteristic of the theatre of the period, and two of them are therefore reproduced in this chapter. The first represents a scene from *Henry VIII,* and the second the scene between Hamlet and his mother, with the Ghost intervening. Hamlet is dressed in a black suit of the period, and has a flowing wig, while his mother might be Queen Anne herself.

The fundamental parts of the men's costume on the stage of Shakespeare's time were the doublet, the tabard, or loose gown with or without sleeves, the short cloak and breeches. The doublet was a close-fitting coat, usually made without sleeves but with overhanging epaulettes. Separate sleeves were fixed to the doublet by means of ribbons with tags of metal. Very often the doublet had a short skirt, and was "pea's cod" or "shotten" bellied. This effect was achieved by stuffing or padding the front part of it. At the time of James I the padding was given up. A ruff or a high collar made of linen, lace, etc., was worn with the doublet. The breeches were very wide, stuffed, and bombasted. Sometimes they were made in Venetian style of loose broad bands decorated with ornaments and gold lace. These were placed over a padded foundation which was very full round the hips and narrow at the knee.

Short breeches were called trunk-hose, and long ones, reaching to below the knee, were known as upper-stocks. Stockings made of cotton, silk, or wool, having patterns on them and clocks at the ankles, were worn over the breeches and gartered under the knee. Long stockings, worn with short breeches, were called trunks, and short stockings, which were worn with long breeches, were known as stocks.

The tabards and short cloaks were made of expensive materials, decorated with lace, embroidery, and even with precious stones. Square-toed shoes, which were made of leather and of various materials, had sometimes high cork soles. The boots had very large tops, which were sometimes trimmed with lace. The hats were of various shapes and dimensions—broad and narrow brimmed, steeple and flat crowned, made of felt and materials in the shape of berets with a stiff brim. In imitation of the gallants, actors used to decorate

HAMLET AND THE GHOST
Nicolas Rowe
1709

HENRY VIII AND WOLSEY
Nicolas Rowe
1709

their hats with ruffs of lace, with gold chains and especially with feathers.

Describing the costume of a smart young landlord, Thomas Middleton wrote: "His head was dressed up in white feathers like a shuttlecock, which agreed so well with his brain, being nothing but cork, that two of the biggest of the guard might very easily have tossed him with battledores, and made good sport with him in his majesty's great hall. His doublet was of a strange cut; and to shew the fury of his humour, the collar of it rose up so high and sharp as if it would have cut his throat by daylight. His wings, according to the fashion now, were as little and diminutive as a puritan's ruff, which shewed he ne'er meant to fly out of England, nor do any exploit beyond sea, but live and die about London, though he begged in Finsbury. His breeches, a wonder to see, were full as deep as the middle of winter, or the roadway between London and Winchester, and so large and wide withal, that I think within a twelvemonth he might very well put all his lands in them; and then you may imagine they were big enough, when they would outreach a thousand acres. Moreover, they differed so far from our fashioned hose in the country, and from his father's old gascoins, that his backpart seemed to us like a monster; the roll of the breeches standing so low, that we conjectured his house of office, sir-reverence, stood in his hams. His cloak of three pounds a yard was lined clean through with purple velvet, which did so dazzle our coarse eyes, that we thought we should have been purblind ever after, what with the prodigal aspect of that and his glorious rapier and hangers all bossed with pillars of gold, fairer in show than the pillars in Paul's or the tombs at Westminster. Beside, it drunk up the price of all my plough-land in very pearl, which stuck as thick upon those hangers as the white measles upon hogs' flesh. When I had well viewed that gay gaudy cloak and those unthrifty wasteful hangers, I muttered thus to myself: 'That is no cloak for the rain, sure; nor those no hangers for Derrick': when of a sudden, casting mine eyes lower, I beheld a curious pair of boots of King Philip's leather, in such artificial wrinkles, sets and plaits, as if they had been starched lately and came new from the laundress's. But what which struck us most into admiration, upon those fantastical boots stood such huge and wide tops, which so swallowed up his thighs, that had he sworn as other gallants did, this common oath, 'Would I might sink as I stand!' all his body might very well have sunk down and been damned in his boots. His spurs looked more like the forerunners of wheelbarrows."

The fundamental parts of a lady's dress in Shakespeare's time were the farthingale, the stiff stomacher, and the ruff or upstanding collar, the first, a very large hoop, either cone-shaped in the Spanish manner or barrel-like "à la française," being worn under the petti-coats and the skirts. During the reign of James I, the farthingale lost much of its wideness. The stomacher or cod-piece was the front part of a tight-fitting, deep-peaked and stuffed-out bodice to the gown. The stomacher was often jewelled, and the bodice was worn over a corset (privie coat) made of bones and buckram and laced at the back. Epaulettes and open falling sleeves were fixed to the bodice, while the actual sleeves had to be tied to it. These were puffed and slashed and usually very big.

> "What's this?" [says Petruchio] "a sleeve? 'tis like a demi-cannon:
> What! up and down, carv'd like an apple-tart?
> Here's snip and nip and cut and slish and slash,
> Like to a censer in a barber's shop."

The ruff and the collar were made of lace, cambric, or linen, and were sometimes so wide as to necessitate the wearing of an "under-proper" made of wire and holland. As head-dress open-work lace bonnets, little hats perched on the top of the head, and felt hats and hoods were in favour. False hair (periwigs), mainly of golden or red colour, was worn and dressed with pearls, tassels, chains, and jewels. The shoes were round-toed and had high cork soles; they were made of leather, velvet, or silk, decorated with patterns and even slashed. The ladies of the upper classes, imitating the Italian coquettes, wore velvet masks in the streets and in the theatres. They used scented gloves, rouge and chalk for their faces.

Although the lace, brocades, and silver and gold of the costumes worn on the stage were usually artificial, the other materials used— silk, damask, and cloth—were most costly. Henslowe's *Diary* and other contemporary writings give us abundant and detailed accounts of the money spent on them.

Among "outlandish" costumes on the Elizabethan stage the Turkish, Moorish, German, French, Spanish, the Janissarian, and even Slavonic garments were known. These of course were rather of a modernized and anglicized character. We know that special costumes were made for such characters as Henry V, Wolsey, Tamerlane, Faust, Tasso, and that stage shepherds wore the Italian "shepherd" costumes described in the next chapter. Henslowe says that the expense of the costumes, which, in most cases, had to be supplied by the actors themselves, caused them great inconvenience, as their salaries were far from sufficient to cover the cost of their stage wardrobes. In fact, the actors' poverty forced them to enter the service of well-to-do members of the nobility and to wear uniformed liveries. This saved them expense, and afforded them the protection of noblemen. Being henceforth regarded as the respectable servants of an aristocrat, they were thus spared the annoyance of being kicked out of towns as pernicious and licentious rogues and vagabonds whenever the local elders or the church authorities did not want them.

The Catholic clergy urged their flocks to attend the ecclesiastical plays as long as they were given in the churches, and also encouraged the production of plays in schools as religious propaganda. Nor did they object, for political and tactical reasons, to Christian protectors of the church participating in the frivolous amateur Court productions. However, as soon as the popular element, real life in the rough, crept into the ecclesiastical plays, the priests pronounced them anathema through fear lest common sense and the live ideas of people expressed amongst the masses in living images would make them doubt the infallibility of the sombre and pessimistic gospel of the church. Even as the Catholic priesthood had been opposed to popular players, farceurs, and clowns, for the same reason it was hostile to the new theatre created by the Renaissance.

Nor did the English Puritans behave any better towards the theatre than the Catholic clergy. Upon the accession of Charles I, but a few years after Shakespeare's death, and only two years after the publication of his works, the drama and music and dancing were, as is well known, one of the first things to be attacked by the Puritans. The appreciation of and interest in the arts and literature—especially in dramatic poetry—which had shortly before risen to an unparalleled height, were stifled in England by main force, and suppressed so quickly and with such ruthlessness that England can scarcely yet be said to have quite recovered from the effects of Puritanical ideology.

Among the many assertions of the Puritans was one to the effect that a poet and a liar were one and the same thing. The Puritans did not distinguish between fiction and falsehood, and the idea was so deeply rooted in their minds that even Davenant, on the occasion of the re-opening of "The Theatre," found it necessary to address his audience on the subject. The Puritans further accused actors of being "roysters, brawlers, ill-dealers, boasters, lovers, loiterers, and ruffians in their life abroad as they were on the stage." Probably they were not far wrong. If modern actors, who are bred amongst more or less cultured people, and who enjoy all the privileges of the intellectual class, are still "in their life abroad," as on the stage, victims of the influence of the motley crowds which constitute audiences, what might be expected of the Elizabethan players? They had to act in inns and theatres, which were "the ordinary places for vagrant persons, masterless men, thieves, horse-stealers, whoremongers, cozeners, coney-catchers, contrivers of treason, and other idle and dangerous persons to meet together and to make their matches." The theatrical managers at the time of Queen Elizabeth had their eyes more on victualling than on art. The taste and behaviour of the Elizabethan spectators could not be compared with that of up-to-date non-committal and well-bred London audiences.

A sonnet which has all the appearance of having been addressed to Shakespeare and Burbage (*Microcosmos,* 1603) says:

> "The stage doth stain pure gentle blood,
>   Yet generous ye are in mind and mood."

Another complaint of the Puritans was that actors appeared in women's attire, and that actresses wore men's garments, although the accusation could not, of course, apply to the English stage at the time, as the first English actress appeared on the stage in 1656, and the first women to appear on the English stage (in 1629) were French. In Prynne's *Histrio-Mastix* (1633) they were denounced as indecent, shameless, unwomanly, and even whores. The London public of the time was apparently of Prynne's opinion, as it gave the unfortunate French women such a hot reception that they had to return in haste to their own country. Queen Henrietta, however, who with her Court ladies was fond of acting, had Prynne fined £5,000 for his writings, ordered his ears to be cut off, and the rest of him to be put in jail. The Puritans stood by the Mosaic law—which they considered binding in the extreme—and this law forbade men to wear women's apparel, it being "an abomination unto the Lord" (Deuteronomy xxii. 5). In *Histrio-Mastix* such masquerading is branded as encouragement to sodomy, and it is stated that "sodomy occasioned by acting in women's apparell, by wearing long compt haire and love-locks . . . Sodomites usually clad their Ganymedes in women's apparell, caused them to nourish, to frizle their haire, to wear Periwigs, and Lovelocks. . . ." In like manner the Puritan Zeal-of-the-Land Busy in *Bartholomew Fair* rages at Leatherhead's puppet-show, and addresses the puppets thus: "Yes, and my main argument against you is, that you are an abomination; for the male among you putteth on the apparel of the female and the female of the male." Whereupon the puppet Dionysius replies: "It is your usual stale argument against the players, but it will not hold against us puppets, for we have neither male nor female amongst us." In the matter of actors wearing female apparel, the Puritans not only objected to men playing straight female parts, but especially to the Travesti plays where situations arose in which the characters of young girls, acted of course by men, changed into men's costumes and vice versa. The Travesti plays were introduced into England from Italy, and were most popular. Heywood, Kyd, Thomas Middleton, Ben Jonson, John Fletcher, and even Shakespeare wrote Travesti plays and scenes.

In spite of the magnificence of the costumes on the Shakespearean stage, the devices for scenic illusion were poor indeed when compared with the mechanical contrivances at the disposal of the modern theatre. As regards the setting for and the presentation of great historical events, such as battle scenes, the stage of that time could only give some symbolical indication of what was taking place. Thus *Henry V* is opened by a chorus with the following apology and request:

> "Can this cockpit hold
> The vasty fields of France? or may we cram
> Within this wooden O the very casques
> That did affright the air at Agincourt?
> O pardon! since a crooked figure may

Attest in little place a million;
And let us, ciphers to this great accompt,
On your imaginary forces work.
Suppose within the girdle of these walls
Are now confined two mighty monarchies,
Whose high upreared and abutting fronts
The perilous narrow ocean parts asunder;
Pierce out our imperfections with your thoughts;
Into a thousand parts divide one man,
And make imaginary puissance;
Think, when we talk of horses, that you see them
Printing their proud hoofs i' the receiving earth;
For 'tis your thoughts that now must deck our kings."

This poetical idea of Shakespeare's is a contrast to Sir Philip Sidney's more critical view of the subject, written about 1593. He says: "Now ye shal have three ladies, walke to gather flowers, and then we must believe the stage to be a garden. By and by, we heare newes of shipwracke in the same place and then wee are to blame, if we accept it not for a rock. Upon the back of that, comes out a hideous monster, with fire and smoke, and then the miserable beholders are bounde to take it for a cave. While in the mean-time, two armies flye in, represented with four swords and bucklers, and then what harde heart will not receive it for a pitched fielde?" The scenic arrangements thus ridiculed are, however, so much an integral part of Shakespearean production during the lifetime of the author, that a short account of them must be given here. Without visualizing the environment of the Shakespearean players, we should not be able to realize the impression which their costumes were producing on contemporary audiences. We shall take the Globe Theatre as representative of the other playhouses.

The two earliest theatres in London—and the first anywhere in England—were The Theatre and The Curtain, both midway between Finsbury Fields and Shoreditch. The earliest-known allusion to

The Theatre is in the year 1576, and to The Curtain in 1577. Neither The Theatre nor The Curtain was used exclusively for theatrical performances, but served also for fencing matches and similar entertainments.

The third playhouse, the Blackfriars Theatre, was erected on the spot where the great religious house of the Dominicans, or Black Friars, had once stood. Shortly afterwards Whitefriars Theatre is said to have been built in Salisbury Court. Then followed the Globe Theatre, the Red Bull Theatre at the upper end of St. John's Street, Clerkenwell, the Fortune Theatre in Cripplegate, the Newington Butts Theatre, and lastly, the Cockpit or Phœnix Theatre. Subsequently there arose other and smaller theatres, the Swan, the Rose, and the Hope, all in Bankside.

The Globe Theatre was at Bankside, i.e. on the south side of the river, and in the immediate vicinity of the Bear Garden. This theatre, in which Shakespeare acted, and in which his dramas were performed, was, like the others, a wooden structure with a straw or thatched roof over the stage (perhaps also over the boxes), which later proved the destruction of the theatre, for on the 29th of June, 1613, during a performance of Shakespeare's *Henry VIII,* it was burnt to the ground as the result of the wadding fired from a gun setting fire to the said roof. The theatre received its name either from its shape or from the figure of Hercules holding the globe at the principal entrance with the inscription beneath—"Totus mundus agit histrionem." Its architectural shape was more oval than circular, in fact, a decided "wooden O." One year after the fire an octagonal structure was erected, yet this cannot have been the last time it was rebuilt, for Hollar's *View of London* in 1647 again describes the building as circular. That part of the house reserved for the audience was separated from the stage rostrum by palings, and by a woollen or silk curtain hung on an iron rod, which was pulled apart from either side. This was the only possible arrangement in those days, for, owing to the thatched roof, or to the fact that some theatres were without roofs, neither curtain nor scenery could be drawn upwards. A balcony ran round the three sides of the building set apart for the public, in imitation of the arrangement in the inn-yards. This corresponds to the boxes of the present day, and was reserved for the more well-to-do portion of the public. There were, it is true, enclosures near the stage, the so-called "Lords' rooms," which are frequently alluded to by the old dramatists, and some theatres had private boxes. Occasionally the seats in the balcony were reserved before the day of a performance. A second or higher balcony was set aside for the orchestra, while the floor of the house was occupied by the "groundlings."

The stage, like the floor of the ordinary dwelling-houses of the time, was usually strewn with rushes, but on special occasions matting was used. At the back of the stage was the well-known balcony, some eight or nine feet above the floor, which served a variety of purposes, and had a curtain which parted in the middle. Below this balcony there was a smaller inner stage also with curtains. It would be from this balcony that Christopher Sly witnessed the play with the disguised page in *The Taming of the Shrew*. It also served for the capitol on which Julius Cæsar was assassinated, it was where the negotiating citizens of Angiers in *King John* entered, and again in the same drama it was from this balcony that Prince Arthur leaped, and by which Romeo climbed to Juliet's chamber. As scenery there were tapestries and curtains and curtain settings, which were set and struck on the outer stage in full view of the audience. Some scenes were indicated by being merely written up on a board, a device still practised at the time of the Restoration.

Most of the methods of staging in use at the time of Queen Elizabeth were retained in England throughout the seventeenth century, although the English theatre was then under the spell of the French. The theatres of the Restoration drama, the old Elizabethan Red Bull, Salisbury, Court, and Cockpit theatres had, with the exception of the balcony, the same arrangements and used the same devices as in Shakespeare's time. The "perspective in scenes" began to appear on the inner stage after 1660. The introduction of painted perspective scenery required much space and a frame, and led to the extension of the inner stage, the shrinking of the Shakespearean front stage, and the borrowing from France of the "picture-frame box stage," which France had borrowed from its inventor Italy.

The performances in Shakespeare's time were given in the afternoons by daylight, hence Shakespeare's public had to dispense with the effects produced by artificial light, at all events in the so-called "public theatres" which were partially unroofed, though the more expensive "private theatres" were completely roofed in. In the production of *Mucedorus* a trumpet sounded thrice as a signal that the play was about to begin, when a flag was hoisted on the flagstaff (the topmost decoration of every theatre), where it remained throughout the performance. At the beginning of the Elizabethan period it was the custom for all the actors to file across the stage in their costumes before the play started—a practice, no doubt, which had come down from the days of the Miracle Plays and Moralities.

The person who read the Prologue in *Mucedorus* appeared in a long black velvet mantle and laurel wreath, i.e. as a poet, probably because the poet originally read the Prologue himself, or at all events because it was read in the poet's name. In Ben Jonson's *Poetaster* and in Shakespeare's *Troilus and Cressida* the Prologue was clad in armour, and in Burnell's *Lagartha* appears as an Amazon.

The clowns, dressed as described later in grotesque "modern attire," delivered improvisations during the performance. In Greene's *Tu Quoque,* published in 1614, we meet with the stage direction, "Here the two talke and rayle what they list"—so little attention had been paid to Shakespeare's exhortation in *Hamlet:* "Let those that play your clowns speak no more than is set down for them." The improvisations of the clown were not in the smallest degree connected with the play itself, but wandered completely away from the subject. In *Mucedorus* an intermezzo of this kind has been preserved, though whether it is the outcome of the clown's improvisation or written by the author for the clown is uncertain.

The incidental music—which Shakespeare made use of extensively and appropriately—was supplied by violins, hautboys, flutes, drums, horns, and trumpets. Music was likewise played during the pauses between the acts, but it seems doubtful whether a curtain was meanwhile let down, or drawn across the stage, for in all the dramas of Elizabethan times the bodies of murdered persons were always carried off the stage by the players on some pretext or other, as they could not be moved out of sight by any other means.

The audience amused themselves during the show by drinking, eating, card playing, and smoking. A German traveller wrote in 1598 that "at the spectacles the English are continually smoking the Nicotian weed, which in America is called Tabaca. They have pipes made of clay, and drawing the smoke into their mouths they puff it out again, along with it plenty of phlegm and deflution from the head. In their theatres, fruits such as apples, pears, and nuts according to season, are carried about to be sold, as well as wine and ale." The young aristocrats who had seats on the stage interfered in the performance and courted the young impersonators of female parts. They were waited upon by the boys belonging to the theatre, who were also employed to applaud.

The performances lasted from two to two and a half hours, rarely for three hours (the time generally specified is "two short hours"), and concluded with a reference to the setting sun and a "Good-night" prayer for the Queen, with all the actors assembled on their knees. At all events, no time was wasted in changing the scene, and the intervals between the acts, if indeed there were intervals, were certainly not long. However, even with the shortest of intervals, *Hamlet* in our day takes almost twice as long as the time specified above, in spite of the many passages omitted when it is played. Hence the only possible conclusion is that the Drama was even more mercilessly cut than it is in our day, and, in fact, we have several proofs that in this respect the plays were treated in the most arbitrary manner. In *Bartholomew Fair* Cokes asks: "But do you play it according to the printed book?" To which Leatherhead replies: "By no means, sir." Cokes: "No! how then?" Leatherhead: "A better way, sir. That is too learned and poetical for our audience." In fact, within the two to two and a half hours, not only was the principal piece itself played through, but the jig was also danced, and if this were one of the longer variety it would sometimes last an hour, as seems evident from Tarlton's *News out of Purgatory*. The jig was danced by the clown, who accompanied himself on the "tabor and pipe."

Richard Tarlton, who died in 1588, was specially famous as a player of jigs, and he may also be called the inventor of the costume of the English clown. The costume of the Fool disappeared in the sixteenth century in England, and was superseded by more realistic attire which allowed the wearer to caricature his own figure or the fashions of the time. As in Tarlton's day, the fashions were Spanish, and men's legs were in tights and short puffed breeches. Tarlton acted in very wide trousers and shoes several sizes too big for him. His head-dress was also too big, and he gave different shapes to it during the show, as well as doing "business" with his pipe and drum. Tarlton was a great favourite with the Court and the populace. He said of himself:

> "He is truely a player-foole,
> And so you may him call.
> You may see his goodly counterfeit
> Hung up on everie wall."

William Kempe, the "Jestmonger and vice-gerent generall to the Ghost of Dicke Tarleton," was Tarlton's successor. He was famous for his improvisations and Moresca dancing, and had given performances not only in England but in Italy and before the German Emperor. Probably Kempe, while giving performances in Italy, saw the *Commedia dell' Arte* players, and borrowed copiously from their costumes to the advantage of his own and that of other English clowns.

The colour of Tarlton's costume is supposed to have been brown or grey. The types created by other English clowns were dressed more or less similarly to Tarlton, and kept to the same principles, but were brighter in colour. The clown, Robert Reynolds, had the enormous shoes and long wide trousers, but carried a wooden sword, and wore a coat with buttons like large balls, both of *Commedia dell' Arte* origin. His tall, white felt hat, decorated with feathers, served the same purpose as that of Tarlton. Another clown, a small man with a large belly, wore a red beard and a costume half red and half yellow which was too small for him, a tiny cloak, a paper collar, and a bonnet with ears attached. Some clowns were in the habit of wearing old-fashioned clothes either too big or too small for them. Following the example of the French clown who dressed as a woman, Dame Perrine, some of the English clowns also appeared dressed as women.

We can well believe that the principles of the costume of English Elizabethan clowns, as well as their manner of acting, were similar to those of the best of our modern versatile clowns, who dress up in exaggerated versions of our everyday dress and perform acrobatic feats, dances, musical turns and gags, either solo or with one or two partners. Possibly the Elizabethan clowns may have been more versatile than those of to-day, yet the Fratellini, Grock, and the late Little Tich remind us of the great craftsmanship of the performers of the *Commedia dell' Arte,* of Tarlton, Kempe, Sackville, Spencer, Reynolds, and other clowns.

Companies of English strolling players, which included clowns, introduced the melodramatic and comic realism of the English stage to the Continent. The English "mises en scène" and Shakespeare became popular abroad, thanks mainly to their efforts. Their style of dress was particularly imitated in Germany, and the English clowns served as types for the German clowns, Pickelherring and Jahn, and the French Jean Potage with his German variation Schampitasche.

CHAPTER VI

THE SEVENTEENTH CENTURY

THE Court Fêtes which kings and princes were in the habit of giving, the mumming and masquerading which these entertainments gave rise to, developed in the seventeenth century into what we now know by the names of Opera and Ballet.

The first opera ever performed was *Dafne,* by Jacopo Peri, with words by Ottavio Rinuccini. It was produced on the 21st of January, 1559, in Florence, in the private house of the Count Jacopo Corsi, and was followed in 1600 by *Euridice,* with Peri's and Caccini's music, and in 1607 by the famous *Orfeo,* with Monteverde's music and words by Alessandro Striggio. The latter is considered the first attempt at musical drama or melodrama, as operas were called at that time.

The musical plays before the time of Peri and Monteverde were as loosely strung together as any other Court entertainments, and consisted of items of music, poetry, dancing, singing, and mime. Later on, "suites" of different dances began to be given as independent shows, called in France "divertissements," and pantomime and "balli" in Italy. It was Mozart and Gluck in the eighteenth century who first gave to Opera the character of a real musical play, and it was Noverre who began to perfect the Ballet and string it together. Even the music of the earliest operas and ballets was undramatic. In these operas there were no arias or duets, but the mimed actions of the players were accompanied and interpreted by ensembles and choruses.

The operas and ballets were acted by amateurs like the other Court shows until 1662. The actors in an opera named *Fedra Incoronata,* produced at the Bavarian Court, were the Kurfürst Max Emanuel himself and the gentlemen of his court.

After the Duke d'Este, considered by some as the founder of

the Italian Renaissance theatre, had begun to produce the comedies of Plautus and Terence in 1466 in the original language at his Court in Ferrara, members of the nobility in Italy and other countries also began to produce Antique tragedies and comedies, as well as plays written in imitation of the Antique by erudite people of the day, pseudo-classic tragedies and *Commedia erudita,* in addition to other Court entertainments. It was also during the Renaissance period that Antique plays began to be acted in the original language by the boys (and sometimes by the girls) in the schools and colleges.

From the tragedies and comedies given at the Courts and in the schools grew the regular dramatic public theatre as we have it to-day.

Of course neither biblical characters nor those of the folk shows appeared in the performances given by the Courts or by the nobility, as they were considered unsuitable for the often licentious genre of the aristocratic entertainment and to the pedantic tone of the erudite play. During the Renaissance on the Continent the theatrical element which appealed most to the populace was in the decaying religious shows and in the grotesque realistic performances given by clowns and troupes of vagabonds and in the Italian *Commedia dell' Arte,* which came to life in the sixteenth century. The latter reached its height in the seventeenth century, and exercised an influence equal to that of the Classics on the writers of regular comedies, the manner of acting, and on the costume of the Comic plays.

During the Renaissance and even later, biblical characters continued to appear in their traditional costumes in schoolboys' performances, in the so-called "School theatre." Moralities were acted in addition to the classic plays by schoolboys and college undergraduates as a means of literary and moral education. The boys, however, did not long maintain in their shows the standard desired by their masters in theology and philosophy, and their performances very soon became mere amusements for themselves, largely influenced by the broad and coarse humour of the popular vagabond players, and very often even of doubtful moral value. As a result of play-acting, German schoolboys of the sixteenth and early seventeenth centuries were becoming, we read, "both immoral and arrogant, and merely learning how to overeat and swill wine." Apparently hot favourites (with the boys, at least), were such "moral" plays as those concerned with Sodom and Gomorrah, and such themes as the seduction of Joseph by Potiphar's wife, etc. But the classics were far from neglected, and served as butts for the wit of the students, who turned out parodies on them.

In England during the reign of Queen Elizabeth boys from the companies of School theatres or, as they were called, "Children's theatres," were often recruited, sometimes even against their parents' wishes, as players of female parts in the professional theatres. The early Children's theatres in England were probably connected with Moralities, which seem to have been acted at St. Paul's and elsewhere by the choir-boys, who gave their performances in their singing school, which was in or adjacent to the church. This led, at the end of the sixteenth century, to the performances being prohibited. In fact, political, ecclesiastical, and literary allusions were indulged in, which may, on the one hand, have sounded more amusing and less mischievous on the lips of children than if they had been spoken by adults, but, on the other, may have been merely a makeshift for the equivocal and lewd jests which it was impossible to put into the mouth of youth. The prohibition seems, however, either to have been withdrawn, or the performances were continued in some other non-ecclesiastical locality, for in 1600 we find that Lilly's *Maid's Metamorphosis* was played by the boys of St. Paul's. The Children's theatres soon came into high favour, especially with the more educated public, and as they were patronized by the Court they very soon grew into an essentially superior institution with quite a hostile attitude towards professional theatres, which were referred to in terms of ridicule and contempt.

Although the Renaissance taught the educated classes of Europe something about dress in Antiquity, and books of travel opened their eyes to the garments worn by Indians, Turks, and even Esquimaux, it was not till the end of the eighteenth century that a definite movement towards the wearing of more or less authentic historical or "etnographical" costume began amongst the actors. The performers in Court shows had been in the habit of acting the majority of parts in the Court dress of their own period or of yesterday. However, to give a touch of local colour or allegorical significance, they would combine "modern" dress with details from Antique or any foreign attire which seemed suitable for the part. To express the Roman cuirass or the naked body, a tight-fitting doublet trimmed with Antique or allegorical ornaments and a short draped skirt or kilt were devised by Italian Renaissance and Baroque artists for male performers in the Court shows. All heroes wore helmets or tiaras decorated with plumes, and tight-laced boots. This heroic costume appeared in different variations, and was used during the seventeenth and eighteenth centuries for the parts of heroes and gods all over Europe, being known in France as the "habit à la romaine," the name given to it at the Court of Louis XIV. The "Oriental" character of any costume during the Renaissance was suggested by a turban. The rest would be a combination of "modern" costume and details from Turkish, Polish, Muscovite, and other dresses. The Turk was in most cases "modern" below the hips, but above would wear a sash and long caftan with Polish galloons on the front. The women's stage costumes in the seventeenth century were even more modern in fashion than those of the men. The ladies who played in the tragedy of the time, just like modern actresses, parted very unwillingly with smart garments of the latest fashions. The etiquette of the Court required performing ladies, except in low-class character, to appear before the kings and princes in Court dress, and this remained for a long time the traditional costume of tragic and ballet actresses. The local colour was suggested merely by ornaments and details.

The conservative partiality for the fashions of the time during the Renaissance and the seventeenth century may be explained by the fact that Court dress with additions of Antique or allegorical decoration was quite adequate for the themes of Court performances and later for the ballets, operas, and the French pseudo-classic poetic tragedies of Rotrou, Corneille, and Racine. Besides, it suited the outlook of the public on the theatre at that time. In those days, for actors and public alike, everything in the theatre was but a fanciful convention. As the scene of the action was merely suggested, so also the historical and local character of a costume would merely be indicated. As the performers of the Renaissance and Baroque theatres played more or less among the public, a certain intimacy between audience and actors was the rule, and the spectators, in such close contact with the players, must have felt to a certain extent as if the latter were some of themselves who were masquerading.

The sixteenth-century performances, except for some Court shows which were given by candle- and torch-light, were nearly always played in the daytime, as had been customary in the Middle Ages. The seventeenth-century performances were given by the dim light of wax candles or oil-lamps. The costumes of these periods could not rely on the deceptive effects arising from artificial coloured lighting, by which cheap material can be made to look expensive and "prop." decorations real, and stage dresses had to be even richer than ordinary garments. Furthermore, people who were accustomed to wear such costumes as not only disguised but even distorted the human figure, could not be induced to appear in the loose and scanty garments and draperies of Antiquity. In authentic Greek, Roman, or even Moorish or Turkish costume, they would have felt, and seemed to others, indecently under-clad or oddly and even comically dressed.

The young ladies of quality of the seventeenth century proudly displayed their breasts with "les tétons en l'air," pressing them upwards and close together by stiff bodices. According to a satirical paper of 1628 they were even ". . . si volages, qu'elles donnaient leur pucelage pour du satin et du velour. . . ." But they would have burned with shame had they appeared in public with bare shoulders or feet. Men, on the other hand, were allowed by Court Etiquette to perform with bare arms and legs, but the torso and feet had always to be covered up. "Cover the arms and legs," says an Italian specialist on theatrical production at the close of the sixteenth century, "with flesh-coloured cloth, but it would not be undesirable to leave the legs and arms bare if the actor be young and handsome, though never the feet."

In the Court shows it was understood that the costume should be in conformity with the etiquette of the Court, not merely similar to that usually worn by ladies and gentlemen of quality, but as luxurious as possible. For instance, " a poor peasant maid" might not appear in a Court production in realistic peasant clothes. She must be dressed "decently," i.e. in velvets and satins, and her social betters, to maintain the necessary balance of class difference, had to wear at least gold brocade or embroidered tissue, and be loaded with jewellery. "I would never dare," says the same expert, "to let a maid appear in a torn skirt. I had better give her a good skirt, and heighten the elegance of her mistress. . . ." The principle on which Court shows were staged appears to have been the richer the better. "The wardrobe of even a poor prince," says the same authority, "would be quite sufficient to dress the most elaborate tragedy. One need only be a man of the world to know how to transform princely clothes, without cutting or damaging them, into the costumes of the Ancients."

In a mythological pageant given by Henri III of France at the Palais de Petit Bourbon in 1581 in honour of the marriage of his leman, the Duc de Joyeuse, to Marguerite de Lorraine, the characteristic touches to the Court dresses of the Naiads, who were played by some of the most noble ladies, were given by the use of heavy silver material decorated with pink and silver crêpe, gold and silver tassels, and diamonds. The dryades were clad in green costumes embroidered with posies of gold flowers and garlands of gold leaves picked out in precious stones, and with large transparent gold silk sleeves over long narrow ones of the same material as the dresses, and had wreaths of gold oak leaves on their heads, over all of which fell gold veils. The hero and heroine of the pageant had gold and silver costumes decorated with precious stones. Mercury wore a costume of flesh-coloured silk, a cloak of gold brocade lined with purple, gilded shoes with wings, and a gilt, winged head-dress. Jupiter appeared in a gold brocade costume of the period, a yellow silk cloak, a scarf embroidered with jewels, and shoes made of gilt leather. Minerva displayed a silver bodice with a bronze head of Medusa on the breast, a golden skirt, and a jewelled silver helmet. In a ballet with music by Monteverde, given at the Court of Mantua in 1608, the ladies playing the "Prudes" (shown in Hell because of their heartlessness) wore smart Court dresses, but in order to emphasize the fact that they were burning in Hell, the material was ash colour ornamented with imitation flames and precious stones sewn on to give the effect of hot coals, while their hair, which, of course, had to be in "artful disorder," was plaited with rubies and garnets, again to suggest glowing embers. When, in 1616, Louis XIII danced the part of a "Fire Demon" in *The Liberation of Rinaldo,* he was clad in a tight-fitting red coat with a kilt cut in points, red tights, a black mask, and a red wig. The gentleman who acted the part of "the Gambling Demon" in the same show had a dress of the period painted over with playing cards and carried a chess-board on his head. The "Spirit of the Air" appeared in a costume consisting of tails and wings of different birds and wore a high hat with long feathers on his head.

The way the sixteenth-century theatre adapted the realistic

costume of the lower orders to the taste of the aristocracy and the manner in which stage folk arranged themselves in "historical" costume may be seen by the following examples. In the Greek Pastorale *Arimene,* produced in the Château de Montreulx at Nantes in 1596, all the performers who appeared as shepherds wore a kind of beautified costume of ordinary sixteenth-century shepherds. They had shorts of silk, cut like those of the peasants, their sleeveless jackets were made of velvet in light "autumn" colours, and the two sheep-skins over these jackets were, of course, finished in a most decorative way. Their staffs as well as their hats were trimmed with ribbons. This "shepherd" costume of the sixteenth century became traditional, and was used on the stage all over Europe even in the nineteenth century with varying modifications.

The "Egyptian Magician," Ciramont, in the same Pastorale, was in a black "Turkish" costume, actually a modified "modern" dress, over which was a long coat with sleeves, and he wore a turban. The Western European peoples became acquainted with the garments of the Turks through the various pictures which began to appear at the end of the fifteenth century after the fall of Constantinople. Since then, up to the nineteenth century, the turban and a long Turkish, Polish, Russian or Hungarian raincoat, usually stylized to suit the taste of the time in which it was worn, became essential to any "Oriental" stage costume.

To what extent the producers of the sixteenth and seventeenth century shows ignored historical accuracy is seen by the following examples. In 1598, in a production of Euripides' *Medea* in Strasburg, the mariners were in knickers and short coats. On the Spanish stage, "Greeks" and "Romans" were to be seen as late as the seventeenth century dressed in the contemporary Spanish fashions. It was quite usual to appear in classic plays with weapons and other accessories of which the Greeks and Romans never had the slightest notion. In the stage directions to his tragedy *Numantia,* Cervantes warns those playing the Roman soldiers not to carry guns, and Lope de Vega expressed surprise at Romans wearing knickers and Turks appearing in Spanish ruffs.

Court shows reached their apex in France in the reign of the "Roi Soleil," Louis XIV, who enjoyed taking part in them himself. The Court entertainments of Louis XIV, as well as the French fashions used in them, were imitated by all other European Courts, and, as far as their means allowed, by the European bourgeoisie.

In 1654, in a ballet entitled *The Marriage of Deleus and Thetis,* the sixteen-year-old king played six different parts—Apollo, Mars, a Dryad, a Fury, a Courtier, and an Academician. It was on this occasion that for the first time ladies took part in a theatrical production in France. The "Apollo" costume of Louis XIV, or "habit français à la romaine," was a tight-fitting "armour" coat of mousseline and precious stones with lace cuffs. Pink tights and laced boots to the knees with red heels studded with stones covered his lower limbs, and on his head was a long and fashionably curled wig and a helmet embossed with rubies and pearls and with enormous white and yellow ostrich feathers and "sunrays." As "Fury," the king appeared in a robe embroidered with tongues of flame and a head-dress of gold snakes and red and black ostrich feathers. The Muse "Erato," impersonated by the Princess Henrietta of England, had a décolleté robe of white satin and gold embroidery with double skirt and long train of Venetian mousseline and double sleeves reaching below the elbows. On her head was a tiara of red and white flowers. Thetis wore a blue dress embroidered with silver ornaments and precious stones, and a feathered tiara, and her décolleté was cut so low that her "seins étaient offert en étalage." Peleus was clad in a similar manner to Apollo, but in brown satin and a short blue kilt (both decorated with embroidered "lambrequins"), with wide blue and white sleeves, over which was a red cloak. He wore white tights and laced boots, and on his head a large blue and white turban with feathers. Neptune appeared in blue satin and diamonds, in imitation of drops of water, a head-dress of silver shells and coral, and blue and white feathers. The "Syrens" had blue bodices, red wings, and long blue skirts with large movable fish-tails on their backs. The Tritons wore the same colours and the same tails as the Syrens, which were attached to their knickers. The allegorical figure of "Surgery" had a bright red costume with "repulsive" surgical instruments hanging at his belt. The gods, Mercury and Jupiter, had costumes similar in cut to that worn by Apollo. Juno wore a dress in the "Spanish" fashion in red material embroidered in black.

At the festivities which were given by the king at Versailles in the summer of 1664 professional actors took part, but after 1670, when Louis XIV, under the influence of his last wife, the bigoted Madame de Maintenon, gave up taking part in the performances, all Court shows in France were suspended. As the whole of Europe imitated France at that time, these shows also ceased at the other Courts, and towards the middle of the seventeenth century the production of ballets and operas fell definitely into the hands of professional players.

The traditional costumes of the seventeenth-century Opera, Ballet, and French pseudo-classic Tragedy were more or less the same as those used in the Court shows. The "habit français à la romaine" was worn by all heroes, gods, and demi-gods. Whether it was Telemachus or Hercules, Catiline or Apollo, the Cid, or a Demon, the dress was the same for all, with the sole difference that the colours and enrichments varied, and that the actors carried different "props" for different parts to symbolize the characters they were playing. In order to balance the enormous Louis XIV wig which was worn with that costume, a short hooped kilt was added to it in 1685.

Among the very few actresses appearing on the stage in the seventeenth century in dresses resembling historical costumes was Mademoiselle Champmeslé, the famous French "tragédienne" and

MADAME CHAMPMESLÉ AS PHÈDRE
IN RACINE'S TRAGEDY OF THAT NAME
1677

pupil of Racine, who wore what nowadays we would call a stylized Roman costume as Phèdre in 1677. She had a long, sleeveless tunic open on the left side so that her leg was bare up to the knee, a cloak with gold embroidered edges, a diadem, and a long embroidered veil.

At the Courts of the kings of England revels and fêtes with guests in masquerade were at one time greatly in vogue. That "Merry Monarch" Henry VIII was very fond of taking part in these shows himself, and his jester and lute-player John Heywood was well known as a composer of comic and satirical one-act Interludes, which enlivened the pauses in the Court masquerades and festivities. Although Heywood was known to be a zealous member of the Catholic Church, his burlesques and farces, such as *The Four Ps* and *The Pardoner and the Friar,* are full of what might to-day be termed "Bolshevik" squibs at the clergy, the veneration for relics, etc. In *The Four Ps* the Pardoner appears with the "All-Hallowes' blessed jaw bone," a "buttock-bone of the Pentecost," and "the Great Toe" of the Holy Trinity, on regarding which latter the Apothecary, another character in the same play, observes that it must be so big either on account of the gout which afflicted the Holy Trinity, or that it must be "a trinity of toes"—"God had made it as big as three toes in one."

English people have always liked not only dressing up but also amateur acting, which is still noticeable to-day, and which accounts for the fact that there are more people in England than in other countries who want to go on the stage. This showed itself by the introduction of acting in the Court masquerades. The simplest form which this took was the presentation of a State visit to some potentate. Surrounded by torch-bearers they paraded before the potentate, masquerading in the costumes of the nobles, princes, and kings of foreign lands, bringing him rich gifts, and entertaining him with dances. Later on dialogue and scenery were added to these perform-

ances by courtiers in Court and fancy dress. In the time of Queen
Elizabeth these Court masquerades became even more popular than
hitherto, and the festivities held in honour of the Queen's visit to
my Lord of Leicester have been described by Scott in *Kenilworth*.
The separate, detached elements of the Court masquerades during
Elizabeth's reign were brought together into coherent form by dramatists like Ben Jonson, Samuel Daniel, John Marston, Middleton,
William Davenant, and others, and gave rise to the English shows
called "Masques." Those shows were partly acted and danced and
partly sung like concert pieces.

Masques developed into brilliant spectacles under Queen Anne
and Henrietta Maria, thanks to Ben Jonson and the architect Inigo
Jones, and remained very fashionable for quite a long time. Even
such a master as Handel, while he was employed from 1717 till 1720
by the Duke of Chandos, wrote music for them. Inigo Jones designed
sets and costumes and devised lighting effects for the masques,
Court pastorals and plays from 1605 until 1640. We still possess
sketches by Inigo Jones for costumes for Ben Jonson's *Masque of
the Fortunate Isles and Their Union,* written for and produced at
Court on Twelfth Night, 1626, which began thus: "His Majesty
being set, enter, running, Johphiel, an Airy Spirit, and (according
to the Magi) the intelligence of Jupiter's Sphere, attired in light silks
of several colours, with wings of the same, a bright yellow hair, a
chaplet of flowers, blue silk stockings, and pumps and gloves, with a
silver fan in his hand." The head-dresses of the characters of Skogan
and Skelton appear to have been the chaperon of the fifteenth century.
Skogan is clad in a short but full-skirted doublet, such as may be
seen throughout that century; and Skelton is enveloped in a long
mantle or gown equally admissible, and wearing the long, upturned shoes of Oriental style which first made their appearance
in Richard II's reign, and towards the close of the fifteenth
century disputed the palm of fashion with the poulaines, or ducks'

bills, and the equally absurd broad-toed shoes which eventually ousted the others. "A Brother of the Rosy Cross" is described by the author as attired "in bare and worn clothes, shrouded under an obscure clothe and the eves of an old hat." He also speaks of his "boots." In Inigo Jones's design for the costume he wears shoes, a doublet with full sleeves, of the pattern of Elizabeth or James I's time, close-fitting breeches, and a very high-crowned hat. In *The Masque of Queens* by Ben Jonson the witches are described by Ben Jonson himself as being "all differently attired; some with rats on their heads; some on their shoulders; others with ointment pots at theyr girdles; all with spindells, timbrells, rattles, or other beneficial instruments, making a confused noise, with strange gestures." The Queen's dresses in the same Masque he speaks of as having "in them the excellency of all device and riches; and were worthily varied, by invention, to the Nations whereof they were Queens." In another of Ben Jonson's Masques, *The Twelfth Night's Revells,* "Oceanus" is described as "naked, the colours of his flesh blew, and shadowed with a roah of seagrenne. His head and beard grey. He is garlanded with sea grasse and his hand sustaynes a trident. Niger in form and colour of an Athirpi blacki: his hayre and rare beard curled; shadowed with a blew and bright mantle; his necke and wrists adorned with pearls, crowned with an artificiall wreath of cane and paper rush. The Masquers, which are 12 Nymphs, Negroes and the daughter of Niger, attended by as manie of the Ocean. The attire of the Masquers is alike in all; their hayre thick and curled upright in tresses, by the Pyramids, but retoorning in the top with a dressing of feather and ferveth. And for the eare, necke and wrist, the ornament of ye brightest pearle. For the light bearers, seagreene, their faces and armes blew. Their hayres loose and flowinge, garlanded with Alga or sea grasse, and yet stucke about with branches of corall and water lillies." Later "the Moone is discovered in ye upper parts of ye house, triumphant in a chariot, her garments white and silver, the dressings of her head antique, and crowned with lights."

Inigo Jones's settings were largely inspired by the famous Italian baroque architects, who began to design scenery for Italian Court shows, Opera and Ballet. From Italy he took the idea of "landschap" and architectural perspectives on painted curtains and "canvas" and of ornamental frames for the shows, from which the much-favoured false-proscenium originated in England. His idea of lighting the stage by lustres hung above the actors and by lamps placed "above the skallop, and round about the sides" and "in the concave, upon the Masquers habits," as well as the use of revolving lights and coloured glass, were also of Italian origin. Besides the above-mentioned lustres the Italian barocco decorators used lamps on the friezes of the settings, discs of lamps at the sides, and a pyramidal arrangement of lamps from above and centre for lighting the stage.

The costumes designed by Inigo Jones were either pseudo-classic in style or inspired by the *Commedia dell' Arte* and other Italian sources. He freely borrowed, with the help of his foreign assistants, from Antonio and Giulio Parigi, the Court artists of the Grand Dukes of Tuscany, and from Callot, and did not escape the French influence of the Louis XIV theatre. The erotic element demanded by the taste of the time was supplied in his men's costumes by their androgynous character, much admired by James I and his son, and in the women's dress by very low-cut bodices which very often displayed the whole bosom. To suit the taste of the Court his costumes were, of course, very elaborate and luxurious. Ben Jonson, speaking of Inigo Jones's men's Greek costumes for the Masque *Hymenaei,* says they were, as was usual at the time, "mixed with some modern additions," and that their tunics were "cut to express the naked in manner of the Greek thorax" (breast armour). He says that the women's dresses had "a very ornamental upper part, a loose undergarment full gathered," beneath which they wore "another flowing garment, which was

TETHYS
Inigo Jones

IRIS
Inigo Jones

round and swelling." On their heads they had coronets, "from the top of which flowed a transparent veil." Inigo Jones's costume for the part of Iris in *Hymenaei* consisted of a long gown in blue and pink with long sleeves and cut so low in front as to come under the breasts, which were covered only with very transparent gauze. Over this gown a bodice was worn with short sleeves of white, patterned with gold and puffed in green and purple at the shoulders. The buskins were white and gold, and the head-dress consisted in trimming the hair with jewelled combs and a curled horn, from which a long buff veil fell behind. On the back were two transparent wings. In the *Masque of Queens,* Penthisilea was in a corselet and dress of deep mulberry and cerulean blue with a fringe of acanthus leaves below the corselet and a classic helmet and lorica. Orpheus was bearded, had a laurel wreath on his head, and a tight-fitting doublet cut low at the neck with long sleeves puffed above the elbows and a loose scarf on the shoulders. His skirt reached to his knees, and on his feet were buskins. The costume for "a Masquer" in Campion's *Lord's Maske* is merely a typical Elizabethan Englishman's dress with the addition of a doublet made in imitation of the "habit à la romaine." The costume for Tethys in Samuel Daniel's *Tethys Festival* (1610) is merely a variation of the ladies' Court dress of the period, but made of lighter material and decorated "in the Roman fashion" with acanthus leaves and ornaments and with shoulder-pieces. The bodice again stops below the breasts, which are covered with transparent material. The lower part of the costume for Ben Jonson's *Chloridia* (1631), with its three-tiered skirt, belongs to the period when the dress was made, but above the waist it is Elizabethan. The bosom is uncovered, and the bodice is cut to follow the shape of the breasts. The same style of bodice is worn by Chloris in the same play, except that the upper part of her gown belongs to the same period as the lower part. The allegorical costumes designed by Inigo Jones do not seem to be very imaginative. "Spring" has a kind of conventional shepherdess's dress with a décolleté again as low as the waist, a small ruff round her neck, puffed sleeves reaching to the elbow, and a short and a long skirt one over the other. She carries a wreath in her hand, and wears another on her head with veil attached. "Disdain" is represented by a woman who wears a bodice with a very low neck, puffed sleeves reaching to the elbow, a skirt of light material which shows the shape of her legs, and is draped on the hips. On the head she wears a diadem with five spear-heads. Jones's "ethnographical" costumes of Poles and Turks, etc., were very similar to each other, and were merely variations of the traditional "Oriental" costume of the Renaissance stage. When Jonson's *The Mask of Beauty* was performed in Whitehall in 1608, the allegorical-mythological characters of the Winds, Vulturnus and Boreas, were clad as follows: the former in a blue robe and cloak strung on wires to give it the appearance of being blown by the wind, a black mask on his face, wings at his back, a sun-disc on his head, and boots of gold. Boreas appeared in bronze-green and white, with grey wings covered with snow and icicles; his shoes were "like snakes' tails," and he carried a leafless branch hung with icicles in his hand. His wig and beard were "awry" and "horrifying," and his cloak was similar to that worn by Vulturnus. The character of "Splendour" had a fire-coloured robe, his chest bare, his fair hair (a wig) hung loose, and in his hand he held a red and white rose. "Perfectio" had a gold dress with a belt inscribed with the signs of the Zodiac, a gold diadem on the head, and held a gold sea compass and an ordinary compass. "Serenitas" appeared in light blue with a long plait, through which a veil of different colours was twined, and as a head-dress had a bright sun-disc with golden rays reaching to the floor. The crowd of dancers, attendants, and others wore bodices and skirts of white and gold, one half of them in cloaks, veils, and decorations of green and silver, and the other in silver and orange. In the Masque called *Love's Welcome,* the character of "Accidence," representing a satire on learning, was dressed in the ordinary costume of a townsman, but his black coat was stuck all over with inscriptions —"Substantivus," "Adjectivus," etc., and the alphabet was scrawled on his hat, stockings, and shoes.

In the classic or fantastic plays of the English Restoration stage the characters were dressed after the traditions established by the Masques and the French pseudo-classic seventeenth-century theatre, while in the "realistic" plays they wore modern dress.

The costumes of the School theatre were similar to those of the Court productions and the Miracle and Morality plays. The public attending the School theatre consisted originally of the upper and middle classes, and was similar in its outlook to that which patronized the Court shows. In their biblical productions the schoolboys and their teachers used the costume of the religious plays, which by this time had become traditional. Christ, God's Mother, God the Father, Angels, Devils, Pharisees, Kings, Queens, etc., appeared as they had been seen on the scaffolds of the later Miracle plays, the Prophets still in their long tunics and short dalmatics over them, and the Patriarchs in the long tunic and cloak. In the classic plays the boys wore pseudo-classic costumes. *Prœnulus* by Plautus was staged in Rome by Canon Inghirami, with a cast of young aristocratic boys who wore most expensive costumes, in which suggestions of the Antique were limited to flesh-coloured stockings and short-laced Roman boots covered with precious stones. The sisters Adelphasium and Anterastylis had cloaks of silver brocade over rich skirts and bodices with wide short sleeves, jewelled chains round their necks, and jewel-studded gold bands encircling their long curled wigs. The pander Lycus appeared in a shirt meant to suggest the long Roman tunic, a long tight-fitting "Oriental" coat of gold brocade, classical helmet on his head and with a sword of which the sheath was gold encrusted with jewels. The servant Milphio was clad in a linen shirt embroidered with black silk over which was a short blue and white striped tunic of taffeta, while the soldier Antamonides (who was followed by two servants, one of whom carried his golden shield and the other his sword) wore a light-blue taffeta cloak lined with gold and fastened on his shoulders by two silver lions' heads studded with pearls, a gold belt, and a plumed helmet. Plautus himself, who appeared as a character in the play, wore a white shirt, gold cloak, a laurel wreath on his head, and carried a book in his hand.

CHAPTER VII

THE *COMMEDIA DELL' ARTE* AND THE COMIC COSTUME IN THE SEVENTEENTH CENTURY

THE costumes of the seventeenth-century Comic theatre were made according to the traditions established by the regular Comedy of the Renaissance and by the improvised *Commedia dell' Arte.*

The Comedies, which were written during the Renaissance in imitation of classic authors, especially of Aristophanes, Plautus, and Terence, were originally acted by amateurs in the classic manner without masks and in pseudo-classic costumes. The "chef d'œuvre" of the whole Renaissance theatre, Nicolo Machiavelli's comedy *La Mandragola,* which was the first to depict the real people of the Italian Cinquecento, and therefore was acted more realistically, was also performed by amateurs, but dressed in modern costumes. The *Commedia dell' Arte* was always acted by professionals, who were representing set or fixed types, and were dressed in costumes of a permanent nature which, like the characters they represented, remained unchanged whatever the play. In contrast to the written comedies, "which could be acted by anybody," the *Commedia dell' Arte* was "a perfect form of theatrical art" and "was not and could not be performed except by professional actors." Originally the performers of the *Commedia dell' Arte* were wandering troupes of comedians, and were acting in the exaggerated realistic manner of the strolling popular players.

"Come entrano guesti dentro a una citta subito col tamburo si far sapere che i Signori Comici sono arrivati, andando la Signora vestita da huomo con la spadi in mano a fare la rassegna, e s'invita il popolo a una commedia, o tragedia o pastorale in palazzo, o all'-hostaria del Pellegrino, ove la plebe desiosa di cose nuove e curiosa per sua natura subito s'affretta occupare la stanza e si passa per mezzo di gazette dentro alla sala preparata, e qui si trova un palco postizzo: una scena dipinta col carbone senza un giudizio al mondo. . . ."

The principal elements in the acting of the *Commedia dell' Arte* were, besides improvising, the action and the movements, and not the words. "Dans ce qui est aux yeux des Italiens le véritable art comique, dans la comédie de l'art, la parole est absolument subordonnée et compte à peine. Aussi quelle source abondante de jeux de scène, de combinaisons ingénieuses, de brusques et saisissantes expositions ils nous offrent."

Scenarii or *soggetti* served as canvas for the acting of plays which had to be improvised by the *Commedia dell' Arte* players before the public.

Of the manner in which such a performance was prepared Evaristo Gherardi, the famous Harlequin of the seventeenth century, tells us in *Le Théâtre Italien:* "Lorsqu'on doit jouer une pièce nouvelle, ou une de celles que l'on remêt au théâtre, ou meme lorsque la troupe est composée d'acteurs qui n'ont pas encore joué ensemble, le premier acteur les reunit le matin; leur lit le plan de la pièce, et leur explique fort au long tout ce qui la compose, en un mot, il joue lui seul devant eux le pièce entière; rappelle à chacun ce qu'il doit dire; lui indique les traits brillant, qui, consacrés par le temps, sont devenus indispensables; les jeux de théâtre que porte la scène et la manière dont les lazis (business and gags) doivent se répondre les uns aux autres."

In the *Commedia dell' Arte,* the players of straight parts—lovers of both sexes (the "innamorata," called Isabella, Lucretia, Ardelia, Lavinia, etc., and the "Innamorato," called Lelio, Fabio, Ottavio, Orazio, Flavio, etc.), and the female servants (Colombina, for instance) usually appeared in the contemporary "street dresses" or "smart get-ups" of the period, while the players of character parts wore special character costumes, funny, grotesque clothes.

All the *personæ* of the *Commedia dell' Arte,* with the exception

PULCINELLA
17th century

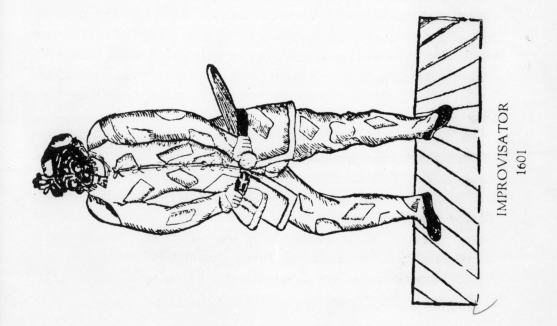

IMPROVISATOR
1601

of the Lovers, originally represented types of different Italian provinces, and the costume of each was typical of a province. As the players of the *Commedia dell' Arte* always presented the same stock characters, and each always played the same type, the realistic provincial costumes gradually became theatrically formalized. The tendency to make the costumes decorative or funny led to exaggerations in form and colour.

Masks and semi-masks were worn by actors playing "character" parts.

The origin of some of the costumes of the *Commedia dell' Arte* certain writers trace as far back as classical Rome, and they see their prototypes in the costumes of the Atellanæ and Mime. Adolfo Bartoli, in his *Scenarii inediti della Commedia dell' Arte,* says that plays in imitation of the Atellanæ were acted throughout the Middle Ages by vulgar histrions, semi-comedians, and semi-acrobats, but "came into great honour towards the end of the sixteenth century." Other and more modern authorities dismiss the classical ancestry of the *Commedia dell' Arte* characters as a myth, and consider them as an invention of the sixteenth century. From my point of view Mime and farcical shows of the Mediæval vagabond players as well as the "Antique and erudite comedies" influenced the scenarii, the manner of acting, and the costumes of the *Commedia dell' Arte.*

The character of the Neapolitan peasant, Puccinella or Pulcinella, Policinella or Pulliciniello (Puccio from Agnello), in the *Commedia dell' Arte* wore long white trousers, a loose white blouse with a heavy leather belt, from which hung a wooden sword and wallet, a scarf round his neck and a high soft hat.

The servants, called Zanni, the simpleton Arlechino and the tyrannical Brighella, representing types from the town of Bergamo, wore uni-coloured masks and headbands or false scalps.

Harlequin, of the *Commedia dell' Arte,* had multi-coloured patches sewn on his breeches and on the long jackets, which were darker in colour than the material of his costume. These represented the patches on the clothes of poor peasants. A wallet and a bat hung at his belt, and the tail of a fox, or of a hare or of a rabbit, which at the time were "stuck on anyone's hat who was the butt of ridicule," and were also worn by some peasants of Bergamo, was fastened to his small cap. Sometimes, instead of these tails, a bunch of feathers was attached to the Harlequin's hat. His mask was brown in colour and made in two pieces, one of which covered the eyes and nose and the other the chin. Both eyebrows and bushy beard on these masks were made of stiff bristles. In the seventeenth century the patches on the Harlequin costume became brighter in colour and triangular in shape, and were joined together by braid. At the end of the same century the patches became diamond shape, and he often wore a ruff collar and a shorter jacket. This costume was retained for the parts of l'Arlequin in the French theatre of the eighteenth century, the players often wearing a three-cornered hat.

Brighella in the sixteenth century wore an olive-coloured half-mask, a kind of livery jacket, baggy trousers with braid along the seams, and a scarf like Harlequin. At his belt hung a purse and a dagger. His hat was a small beret. During the seventeenth century his coat became white with a turned-down collar. Brighella's brother Fenocchio and other servants like Scapino, Mezzetino, Franca-Trippa, Trivellino, Coviello, Gandolin, Turlupin, Bertolino, and Buratino wore costumes similar to that of Brighella.

The players of the Venetian character Pantalone, or Pantaleone, also called il Magnifico—an avaricious and conceited old man—and of certain other characters like, for instance, the original Arlechino, often appeared in the earlier period of the *Commedia dell' Arte* with a large exposed phallus like the Antique comedians.

The earlier costume of Pantalone consisted of tight-fitting long red trousers or red breeches and stockings, a short, tight-fitting jacket, similar to that of Brighella, a loose, long black cloak with

PANTALONE
Callot

plain sleeves, red bonnet, and yellow Turkish slippers. He wore a half-mask with a long nose and a long pointed beard. At his belt was often stuck a dagger, a large folded handkerchief, and a purse. At the loss of Negroponte by the Venetians Pantalone changed the colour of his legs from red to black as a sign of mourning.

The Doctor, called Graziano, Balogardo, Balanzone, etc., a type from Bologna, the town of learning and good food, usually wore, like Pantalone, a grey beard and a black or flesh-coloured mask covering his nose and forehead. In the sixteenth century his black costume was a skit on the dress of the learned members of the University of Bologna. He wore a long jacket with a black cloak over it, which reached to his heels, black shoes, stockings, and breeches, and a small black beret. In the middle of the seventeenth century one of the celebrated actors of the part, Lolli, added a wide ruff round the neck to the costume of the Doctor, and began to wear a very wide-brimmed felt hat. Other interpreters of the Doctor's part elaborated his costume still more, but its basis remained always the same.

The Capitano of the *Commedia dell' Arte* was the braggart warrior of the Antique popular farces, the "Miles Gloriosus" of Plautus. As the Captain was merely a satire on the military profession, his dress followed the contemporary changes of military uniforms. His mask was originally skin-coloured, and had a long nose. He wore a helmet or hat with feathers, and carried a long sword. After the fifteenth century the Spaniards were considered particularly belligerent, pretentious, and boastful, and in the sixteenth century the Captain was often arrayed in the Spanish military costume with an exaggerated ruff round his neck and small Spanish beard. Sometimes his costume was striped. Giacomo Callot, in his drawings, represents the Captain in a small hat with long feathers, usually with a small tabarro, in tight-fitting breeches and stockings or tights, and with a wooden sword. There were a number of terrifying names attached to the part of Captain, such as Capitano Spavento della Valle Inferna, Rodomonte,

Rinoceronte, Cocodrillo, Matamoros, Sangue y Fuego, and Spezzafer. There were also many variations of the type of the Captain, such as Giangurgolo, Vappo, Pasquino, Pasquariello, etc. The German version of the type was called "Horribilibifrax," and the most famous French were Crispin and Scaramouche. In France the latter was modelled by the famous actor Tiberio Fiorilli—who, according to legend, taught Molière to act—on the Italian type of the Neapolitan Captain Scaramuccia. In Italy this roysterer was always dressed in black and wore a mask. Fiorilli put aside the mask so that he might display his talent for making grimaces, and appeared with his face powdered.

"Cet illustre comédien
Atteignit de son art l'agréable manière.
Il fut le maître de Molière
Et la Nature fut le sien."

The type of Crispin was created in France by the actor Raymond Poisson, and as in the case of Scaramouche was no longer representative of brawlers and fighters but was merely a valet. The typical parts of his costume were an enormously long sword and Spanish funnel boots.

The character of Pedrolino, Piero or Pierro, from which developed the French Pierrot, was originally a servant, but being young and handsome he also played the part of lover to the women-servants and soubrettes. His costume originally was very similar to that of Pulcinella, and became in the eighteenth century what we see in the pictures of Watteau. Pierro played without a mask, but with heavily powdered face. The Italian Pagliaccio and the French Paillasse were two variations in the later period of the type of Pierro. In the nineteenth century in France the costume of Pierrot was worn, although transformed by the famous pantomimist Jean Gaspard Baptiste Debureau. Debureau was engaged in 1817 when a boy with his family at the Théâtre des Funambules du Boulevard du

Fortuna per despett
Me fec, volar la robba co i dinar,
La patria abbandonar,
E de CARLO CANTV me fec BVFFETT.
Ma pò mudò concett.
Quando da ZAN me mess a reui
Come CARLO incontrai fortuna au
Come BVFFETT. la prouo a la
rouersa.

BUFFET

17th century

Temple in Paris to do acrobatic exercises on tight-rope and carpet. Later on the director of this theatre made him act in one-man panto-mime in the style of the old *Commedia dell' Arte*. In these shows he wore a loose white blouse with a low-cut neck, long trousers, a white make-up, and a black skull-cap. Debureau died in 1846.

The French nineteenth-century symbolists and Montmartre artists, like Willette, re-endowed the character of Pierrot with the same cos-tume as he wore in the time of Watteau, and towards the end of the nineteenth century he became a "sans-souci" Bohemian, a senti-mental or disappointed dreamer, and even a "fin de siècle" neuras-thenic and a symbol of death.

"Ce n'est plus le rêveur lunaire du vieil air
Qui riait aux aïeux dans les dessus de porte;
Sa gaîté, comme sa chandelle, hélas! est morte,
Et son spectre aujourd'hui nous hante, mince et clair.

"Et voici que parmi l'effroi d'un long éclair
Sa pâle blouse a l'air, au vent froid qui l'emporte,
D'un linceul, et sa bouche est béante de sorte
Qu'il semble hurler sous les morsures du ver.

"Avec le bruit d'un vol d'oiseaux de nuit qui passe,
Ses manches blanches font vaguement par l'espace
Des signes fous auxquels personne ne répond.

"Ses yeux sont deux grands trous ou rampe du phosphore,
Et la farine rend plus effroyable encore
Sa face exsangue au nez pointu de moribond."

(PAUL VERLAINE.)

The French theatre of Molière in the seventeenth century, which set an example to the comic stage all the world over, used for the farcical characters more or less the same kind of costume as did the *Commedia dell' Arte* for its character types. Of course, Molière's Court shows, divertissements, ballets, and plays, like

Amphytrion and *Psyche,* were dressed in the "pseudo-classic" tradition, and his "character comedies" like *Tartuffe* in the costumes of his time. The principles of the *Commedia dell' Arte* also influenced the actors' costume in the French Théâtre de la Foire, from which grew the French Comic Opera. But Molière's actors did not make use of masks, whereas the players of the Théâtre de la Foire wore them for certain parts. When the latter began to act their shows to the accompaniment of songs sung by special singers, and thus created a new "genre" of show called Vaudeville, the habit of wearing masks was dropped. "Les Forains," Lesage tells us, "voyant le public gouter ces spectacles en chansons, s'imaginèrent avec raison que si les acteurs chantaient eux mêmes les vaudevilles, ils plairaient encore d'avantage. Ils traitèrent avec l'Opéra qui, en vertu de ses patentes leur accorda la permission de chanter. On composa aussitot des pièces purement en vaudeville et le spectacle prit alors le nom d'Opéra-Comique." The Opéra-Comique which developed from Vaudeville was also played without masks.

MASK WORN BY COVIELLO

CHAPTER VIII

THE EIGHTEENTH CENTURY

THE beginning of the eighteenth century brought very little that was new to the theatrical costumes inherited from the seventeenth century and adopted by the theatre throughout Europe.

The Paris Opera House faithfully followed the old traditions, using magnificent perspective scenery, various machines for scenic effects, and dressing its singers and dancers in the elaborate "habits à la romaine," "habits de cour," etc. The most astonishing anachronisms in costume were quite customary, and it did not surprise a French audience in 1700 to see the gods of Olympus flying on ropes, which were "visible from the third box," among canvas clouds, got up in embroidered velvets, silks, and powdered wigs. In dramatic operas, then known in France as "tragédies lyriques," and in ordinary drama at the opening of the eighteenth century, kings, tyrants, and heroes wore brocade doublets with short ornate skirts, similar to curtain pelmets, or short "paniers," ribbons on the shoulders, and lace round the neck. Their cloaks were velvet, their wigs, with pig-tails beneath plumed hats, were elaborately curled, and it was the rule to appear on every occasion wearing white leather gloves and using handkerchiefs and snuff-boxes. Operatic and Ballet queens, princesses, fairies, and nymphs wore silk brocade or velvet Court dresses with sleeves tight to the elbows, had long waists, and were freely adorned with fringes, ruffs, and lace. They were usually escorted on the stage by little pages, whose business it was to arrange the long trains of the dresses. As queens had the right to two such trains, two pages were attached to each of them. "When the scene was emotional the boys were forced to run after their mistresses, following their movements with great rapidity." Female dancers

121

appeared in dresses reaching to the ankles, and male dancers in the same costume as operatic singers, with masks and high wigs. The only difference, for instance, between the demons' and the tritons' costumes in the ballets was that the first were made of "fire colour" and silver, and the second of green and silver. Of course, the traditional "shepherd" costume and the "Oriental" costume were still in use in Opera and Ballet, as well as various allegorical adaptations of Court dresses.

At the dramatic Théâtre Français classical heroes appeared in curled and powdered wigs, and in the same type of luxurious costume as the operatic singers and ballet dancers. Cæsar and Œdipus made their appearance in the carefully arranged and powdered "perruque carrée" and three-cornered hat with plumes, which in the eighteenth century took the place of the plumed tiara of Louis XIV's time. Plumes on hats reached such a height that they "mettaient les acteurs souvent dans le cas d'éteindre les lustres ou de crever les yeux à leurs princesses en leur faisant révérence." The masses of plumes on the actors' heads made them look like cavalry horses on parade. "L'acteur Dufrenne, dans Gustave, sortait des cavernes de la Dalécarlie superbement empanaché, habit bleu céleste à parements d'hermine, et Sarrazin s'écriait couvert d'un habit de brocart d'or, sous les lambris d'un palais de Golconde:

"La nature marâtre en ces affreux climats
Ne produit au lieu d'or que du fer, des soldats."

As was already common before the eighteenth century, actors got up to their eyes in debt through their passion for luxury and through trying to gain the adulation of the public by richness of costume. An actor named Vanhove ruined himself on costumes for the parts of kings which it was his job to play at the Théâtre Français. One of his suits of armour, which was made of green velvet embroidered with "a gold trophee composed of canons, drums, and guns" in

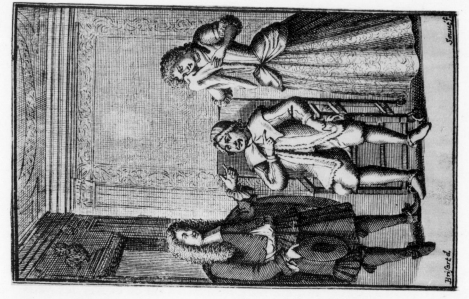

COSTUMES OF MOLIÈRE'S
'LE MALADE IMAGINAIRE'
17th century

COSTUMES OF MOLIÈRE'S
'LE MISANTHROPE'
17th century

which he "contrived to have two pockets, one for his handkerchief and the other for his snuff box," cost him about fifty pounds.

In the first quarter of the eighteenth century tragic actresses began to wear costumes of the period instead of Court dress. The theatre from that time not only strictly followed the constantly changing "mode," but often even created the fashions for the "dames de qualité" of the town and for the Court.

In the eighteenth century it was said that a fashion scarcely lasted longer than a flower, and "la mode" became a veritable demon which tormented the whole world. The humblest grisette or a poor working woman in Paris indulged in quite elegant fashions, and aimed, above all, at "faire petit pied." Dufresny compared women to amusing birds which changed their plumage two or three times daily, and remarked that the disdain felt by all honest women for their less moral sisters did not prevent the former from imitating the mode of dress of the latter. Some time before the Revolution, Mercier, in his *Tableau de Paris,* stated that even the women of the lower classes often displayed an impudent luxury in their toilettes. "Women," said he, "show no restraint in this matter; they wear just what they choose. The wife of a clerk or a grocer goes about dressed up like a duchess, but the authorities don't interfere. A person may display the most unbridled luxury, but as long as the royal imposts and poll-tax are paid, she is quite free to ruin herself."

When about 1718 the "paniers" (or hoops) began to be worn by women in everyday life, they were immediately introduced on the stage. There were different kinds of hoops, being of various shapes and purposes. The pocket-hoop, which was used in the morning, was like a pair of small baskets worn on the hips. The bell-hoop (for the so-called "robe de ville" or afternoon frock) was a petticoat shaped like a bell, and made with cane and rope for framework. According to an English contemporary, a lady walking in such a hoop in the street was "filling up the whole footway with her stately and voluminous person." The full-dress hoop (for the "robe habillée" or "robe de Cour") was a straw petticoat. It was so enormous that "people saw one half of it enter the room before the wearer." In going through a narrow passage the lady had to tilt the hoop and carry it under her arm, exhibiting a "show petticoat" below it and "a pair of round calves" in embroidered thick silk stockings. "Such care was taken of appearances that even the garters were worn fine, being either embroidered or having gold and silver fringes and tassels." Hoop-petticoats at the beginning were worn by rich women only, but later, thanks to the ingenious invention of a French dressmaker, Mademoiselle Margot, who devised a method of producing them cheaply, they became quite popular. The stays worn with the hoops were made very long, and had to fit so tightly that the wearer had to hold on to the bedposts while the maid was lacing her. The bodice worn over the stays was stiffened with whalebone. Its sleeves fitted the arms, but had wide cuffs which were sometimes made like funnels—"en pagode." The powdered hair, though at first worn low, and drawn up from the temples and forehead, began to be dressed high towards 1750. This coiffure was decorated with ribbons, feathers, flowers, jewels, and even with birds and ships, and gradually reached an enormous height. We read that when Marie Antoinette passed along the Great Gallery at Versailles amongst the assembled crowd a regular forest of feathers was seen moving above the heads of the people.

In 1727 Court dress was again introduced in Tragedy at the Théâtre Français by two well-known dramatic actresses, Dangeville and Adrienne Lecouvreur, in the parts of Ericine and Talestris.

These two ladies were two of the five brightest luminaries of the Théâtre Français of the eighteenth century. The others were Dumesnil, Gaussin, and Clairon. The story of Lecouvreur is well known. Mademoiselle de Dangeville, described as an extremely good-looking woman, played the parts of young soubrettes for

BALLET COSTUME
Paris Opera
18th century

'AFRICAN' BALLET COSTUME
Paris
18th century

thirty-three years, i.e. until she was forty-nine, "with a truthfulness and subtlety which united all votes in her favour." Mademoiselle Dumesnil, when she was not as drunk "as a coachman," had no rivals for "majestic, furious, daring movements, for brilliance of voice, pauses, and nuances." Mademoiselle Gaussin "was just Mademoiselle Gaussin in everything she acted," and was famous for having 1,372 lovers, most of whose names were well known to the public at the time. Mademoiselle Clairon "despised the natural" on the stage, and her acting was "le plus achevé de l'art." She was the chief heroine of the troupe at the Théâtre Français, but was often indisposed and acted but seldom. When reproached by the management because she appeared at such long intervals, she invariably replied that one of her performances was sufficient to keep the Théâtre Français going for a month. There were critics, however, who did not hold as high opinion of her as an artist as she did herself, and considered that her acting was only worthy "of some consideration," whereas by nature she "was infamous, false, and hypocritical." She was small, but on the stage appeared tall with "eyes full of fire and which breathed voluptuousness; she had beautiful teeth, her bosom was well moulded; she had a modest air, a sparkling temperament, and sweet and engaging conversation. . . . Looking at her, one experienced a pleasure which the other senses were anxious to share." Her vanity and arrogance, which were probably the result of the adulation of her many lovers (amongst whom were princes, dukes, and nobles, members of the Parlement, Army officers of high rank and others of lesser degree), were notorious, and in strong contrast to her charming physique. To Mademoiselle Clairon's efforts is due the reform of the traditional woman's tragic costume on the French stage.

A new variation of the traditional man's costume, i.e. of the "habit à la romaine," was introduced at the Théâtre Français by the famous actors Baron and the Dufresnes, who invented a doublet of velvet, and wore breeches and stockings with garters instead of tights. The "habit à la romaine" in this new form was used by generations of actors for any outlandish tragic character.

The players of Le Théâtre Italien (*Commedia dell' Arte*) which, since the end of the seventeenth century, had been in great vogue in Paris, brought with them from Italy the tradition of appearing in stereotyped costumes and masks. Only "lovers" played without masks and in the dress of the time. The example of Le Théâtre Italien influenced the other Parisian Comedy and Vaudeville theatres, where comic characters appeared in costumes taken from the *Commedia dell' Arte* players, lovers in "habits de ville," and maid-servants, called "soubrettes," in hoop-petticoats and the latest fashions of the period, and peasant women and girls in "nicely" made and unobjectionable rustic costumes of picturesque cut and colour and in fancy dresses of "shepherdesses."

In those days actresses who played the parts of "soubrettes," and even some of the tragediennes and cantatrices, were nearly all kept by aristocrats or rich men, and from vanity would not appear on the stage in anything but smart and provoking frocks. For the same reason they used so much paint on their faces, especially white and pink, that "their complexion was like that of young milkmaids." In a comedy it was quite usual to see an actress who possessed a rich lover playing the part of a servant and dressed in much richer style than her mistress, or in a tragedy to see the leading actress in a Court dress and the others in old costumes of the preceding century from the theatre wardrobe.

An exact idea of what the costumes of the French Comedy stage of the eighteenth century were like can be gained from two paintings of Watteau, in whom the whole spirit of that age seemed to be embodied, known as "Les Comédiens Français" and "Le départ des Comédiens Italiens," from "La Marche Comique" of Pater, "Le Polichinelle" and "La Camargo" of Lancret, from the portrait by Sicardi of the actor Préville in the rôle of Mascarille, and from numerous other pictures in which are seen many of the characters of the French comic theatre, such as Pierrots, Harlequins, Columbines, Scapins, Mezzetins, Doctors, etc. Without doubt the work of Watteau and that of his pupils and followers, Pater, Lancret, Louis and François Watteau, de Lille, Huet, and Fragonard, influenced the eighteenth-century comedy stage all over Europe.

Neither the travestis costume nor the travestis plays were any longer in fashion in the eighteenth century. Mademoiselle Raucourt, who in her private life had a strongly masculine disposition, appeared in one play as a man, but was booed. "This essay seemed most daring, although it failed to create an illusion. Some people, perhaps, might have believed she was a man, but others had strong reasons to be assured of the contrary."

There was one type of costume especially favoured on the eighteenth-century French stage. This was the so-called "Spanish" costume, which followed the original Spanish fashions of the end of the sixteenth and beginning of the seventeenth centuries. It was worn in the "cloak and sword" plays by the characters of Spanish and Italian origin. For men it usually consisted of a doublet, short hose or trunk hose, both heavily adorned with puffs, a ruff-collar, a short cloak, and a plumed hat. The eighteenth-century Spanish stage costume for women was made of soft materials with an upstanding "Medici" collar. Guiard painted the portrait of Madame Elisabeth, the sister of Louis XVI, in a costume of this sort, and Greuze immortalized the French "Spanish" costume for men in his picture of Monsieur de Boisset.

The reform of the pseudo-classic tragic costume in France was advocated by Diderot, Marmontel, and Voltaire, whose *Encyclopædia* began to appear in 1751. Before these, in 1730, in Germany, a certain Professor Gottsched raised his voice on behalf of the "accurate imitation" of historical truth on the stage. The actress Karoline Neuber, who in the ordinary way considered "the matter of costume unimportant and not worth spending money on," wishing to do the professor a bad turn as the result of a private quarrel, appeared in 1741 in one of his plays in the part of Cato wearing "a true copy of the Roman dress," and succeeded in her object, inasmuch as the public jeered and the professor's play was a failure.

A French actress, Mademoiselle Favart, began to reform the traditional costumes of the Comedy and Vaudeville stage. She was an intelligent woman of good taste, and the wife of the famous writer of comedies and books for comic operas, who, as rumour goes, only put his name to them while she was the real author. Mademoiselle Favart thought that an actor should be dressed, not by tradition, but according to the demands of the character he was interpreting. In 1761, considering it "very unsuitable for a Turkish princess to wear a modern dress with long train," she appeared in one of her husband's comedies, *Soliman le Second ou les Sultanes,* in a real Turkish woman's dress which "excited the extreme surprise" of the spectators. Later, in *Les Amours de Bastien et Bastienne,* in the part of the peasant Bastienne, instead of appearing as was usual in a "shepherd" costume, i.e. a panier with diamond ear-rings and white gloves, she wore a plain white cotton dress, her hair dressed flat and unpowdered, a small gold cross at her throat, and peasant's "sabots."

While Mademoiselle Favart was active in the French Comic theatre, the tragedian Lekain (or Le Kain), who, with Grandval, Bellecour, Préville, and Brizard, was one of the greatest male stars of the day at the Théâtre Français, was trying to reform the tragic costume at his theatre. His efforts to substitute "des habits appropriés aux temps et aux mœurs, aux quels appartenait l'action réprésentée" for the traditional pseudo-classic garb were by no means revolutionary in nature, but at the time seemed most·daring. Lekain's new costume for the part of Genghiz Khan in Voltaire's *L'Orphelin de Chine* in 1755 consisted of a "soubre-veste de satin rose sèche, un manteau de soie cramoisie à ramages, broché en or, et doublé de satin tigre. La coiffure était

SPANISH COSTUME

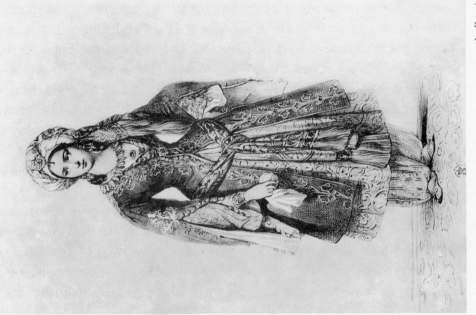

COSTUME OF ROXANE

formée d'un bonnet orné de plumes d'autruche, et ceint d'un diadème qui semblait se rattacher a un muffle de lion. Les cheveux dessinés en bouche sur les oreilles, se relevaient en chignon derrière la tête. Enfin l'acteur tenait dans sa main un arc doré et portait sur son dos un carquois doré, rempli de flèches dorées aussi." It was a sort of new and fantastic adaptation of the Oriental costume to the established traditions of the "habit à la romaine," which had very little that was "historical" about it. Lekain's "Antique" costume was no less fantastic. As the "sweet" Antiochus, he wore a tunic of white satin decorated with little flowers and lined with bottle-green material, breeches of cream-coloured silk, blue stockings, yellow shoes with red heels, and a cloak of purple velvet edged with fur and decorated with gold. Lekain even dared to go so far in his "realism," "in imitation of the English," as to appear with arms covered with blood when coming out of his mother's tomb in the part of Ninus.

Lekain was assisted in his efforts to reform the pseudo-classic tragic costumes by Mademoiselle Clairon, who was encouraged by her friend Marmontel. In Voltaire's *L'Orphelin de Chine* she appeared without paniers and with bare arms.

To Clairon's efforts, by the way, is due the fact that after the Easter holidays of 1759 the stage of the Théâtre Français was cleared of those aristocratic spectators who had always been wont to sit on either side of the actors.

Clairon acted the part of Roxane in a stylized Turkish costume, "en sultane," and even dared, in spite of laughter, to appear as the distressed Dido clad only in a "chemise" and with hair dishevelled. She also fought against the traditional manner of making up the face too white. "Such a tint," she said, "by which nobody is deceived and against which people of taste murmur, makes the skin coarse and yellow, dulls the brightness of the eyes, and makes rings round them, deadens the precious mobility of the features, and is in continual contradiction to what the public hears and sees."

After the retirement of Clairon and the death of Lekain, other actors began to follow their initiative. But although Lekain's Genghiz Khan and Antique costumes very soon became traditional, the ideas of Clairon were too advanced, and did not appeal sufficiently to the vanity and conservatism of the women of the period to conquer the stage too quickly.

Although the theatre in England in the eighteenth century was the slave of French ideas in the matter of costume, the realistic Elizabethan traditions were still alive, but with certain modifications due to the precious manners of the time. We can see, from the dresses worn by Garrick, Mrs. Siddons, and others, how realism in costume was understood in England in the eighteenth century. The first named did not trouble about historical accuracy in his costume, but for the sake of realism, and to get his heroes over to the public with more ease, he acted in "modern dress," adapting it to suit the character he was playing. When he appeared as Romeo with Miss Bellamy he looked like a young Englishman of the eighteenth century. As Hamlet he wore the same, but in black; as Lear he had added to the dress of the period a short cloak lined with ermine, and as Macbeth he was in scarlet, red, and cerulean blue. When playing an ancient Greek, Ægis, in 1758, he wore the costume of a Venetian gondolier, on the ground that the majority of Venetian gondoliers at that time were of Greek origin. In the part of Richard III, in which he made his début in 1741, he wore what was known as the "Spanish" costume. The English tragic actresses of the eighteenth century wore modern dress with additional "characteristic" details. Medea wore a striped "Turkish" turban with long ends hanging over her loose hair, Lady Macbeth had jewels and feathers in her hair, Juliet wore a veil, and Hermione had a cross at her neck and a cloak over her head.

A great follower of Garrick's ideas on costume was Dalberg, the director of one of the best theatres in Germany at Mannheim. To

GARRICK AS KING LEAR

The Enthoven Collection

him, and to the famous Iffland, an actor and régisseur of his company and later director of the Berlin National Theatre, is due the reform "à la Garrick" of German theatrical costume. Like Garrick, Iffland considered the characteristic and typical touches of the part, and not history, as essential in theatrical costume. As Pygmalion he wore an elaborate silk cloak. Speaking of the necessity of truth in stage costume, he expressed the opinion that the prettiness of the dress should be considered first.

When in 1792 Iffland was appointed régisseur of the Court and National theatre at Mannheim, he wrote in the *Kleidungs-Reglement* for the actors: "Mannistfaltigkeit und Unterschied der Kleidungen, nach Verhältniss und Standesabstuffung ist auf dem Theater—eben so wesentlich, als im gemeinen Leben. Auf dem Theater, darf hie und da, mit achtung jedoch der Wahrheit im ganzen, die Niedlichkeit, der Wahrheit vorgezogen werden—oder eigentlicher—sie soll der Wahrheit zur Seite gehen.

"Die Aktrizen, welche die Soubretten spielen, gehört, wenn ihre Dame in ganzem Anzuge spielt, ein aufgezogenes nicht garniertes einfaches Kleid, durchaus kein Huth nochweniger em Modeaufsatz, in Flor oder Attlass mit bunter Aplicatur, sondern blosser Kopf, oder etwa, nach der Art wie man sie jetzt trägt, eine Schlaüffe oben in das Haar. Ein Huth Kann nur gestattet werden wenn die Dame auf Reisen wäre, und dann ein enfacher Huth. Spielt die Dame in halben Anzuge, so kann die Soubrette etwa ein Caraco tragen, aber nicht garniert. Einfache Schürze, Keine Ringe. Die Aktrizen welche Bauerinnen spielen, tragen: In keinem Falle Attlass, noch Attlass Hüthe, oder Hüthe mit hohem Kopf; auch, wenn es nicht erwiesen, reiche Pachter, oder Gemeinds Obrigkeiten sind—Seide und dann nur die Leibgen, keineswegs aber die Röcke; keine grosse Bouquette auf den Hüthen und am Busen."

Apart from the ordinary modern dress, the "habit à la romaine," the "Turkish," and the "Spanish" (which Iffland called "die altdeutsche Kleidung") costumes, he very seldom resorted to the dress of other periods and peoples. Women appeared in Iffland's productions mostly in the contemporary fashions with "historical" details added or stylized according to the epoch of the play. Modern plays were acted in the eighteenth century in Germany in realistic contemporary dresses. Examples of such can be seen in the drawings of Chodowiecki for Lessing's *Minna von Barnhelm* (1770), Schiller's *Raübern* (1783), and *Kabale und Liebe* (1786).

It was Talma who revolutionized theatrical costume in France. It was in the tragedy of *Brutus* in 1789 that he appeared for the first time in historical Roman costume with bare arms and legs, on which occasion the public, and above all the actors, were much shocked. In his *Memoirs* Talma explained his ideas on theatrical costume.

"Truth in the costume as well as in the scenery," he says, "increases the illusion, takes the spectator right into the century and the country where the characters are living. Realism in dress helps the actor to give each of his characters a different physiognomy." Saying that the theatre should give a live history to young people, he accused those who distort history on the stage. "I remember well," he continues, "that in my young days when I read history I imagined princes and heroes to be just as I saw them on the stage. I saw Cæsar dressed in tight-fitting white satin with a long chevelure tied with bows and ribbons. If an actor occasionally appeared in a costume which resembled the antique, he always spoilt it by covering it with ridiculous embroideries, and I believed that silks and velvets had been worn as much in ancient Athens and Rome as they were in modern Paris and London."

Talma, who was a friend of the painter David, and who was himself something of an artist, studied Antique art, and his costumes for tragic parts were copied from Greek and Roman sculptures. "I had many obstacles and prejudices to overcome, less from the public than from theatrical folk, but in the end success crowned my efforts.

Lekain could not have overcome so many difficulties in his day; the moment had not then arrived. Lekain did everything it was then possible to do, and the theatre should be grateful to him. It was he who took the first step, and the fact that he dared made us more daring later."

In 1775 the actress Charlotte Brondes appeared for the first time in Germany in a Greek costume, but Greek only as regards detail, and her example was followed by the actresses Koch, Seyler, Karoline Doebbelin, and others.

At the Paris Opera costume innovations began to be timidly introduced in the middle of the eighteenth century. Sophie Arnould, the famous cantatrice—more famous on account of her extraordinary success in advancing her career by her wits and of her adventurous amours than on account of her voice—used to appear in "classic" operas in the ordinary dress of the period. Her contemporaries said of her voice that it was "the most beautiful asthma ever heard to sing," and were not exactly flattering to her physique, mentioning the fact that her skin was "extremely dark and dry," and that "she always had her mouth full of saliva," and while talking "she sent the cream of her speech into your face." When somebody preached morality at her she replied that "women only give themselves up to God when the devil doesn't want them any longer."

The first woman who dared to appear in an opera with bare arms and legs was the all-powerful Mademoiselle Huberty. In Marmontel's and Piccini's Opera *Dido* she wore a costume designed for her by Moreau after antique Roman bas-reliefs. Her loose tunic of fine linen was fastened with a belt beneath her bosom; over the tunic was a purple cloak; laced sandals were on her bare feet; and she had a crown on her head with a long veil attached to it. Before Mademoiselle Huberty, a singer, Louis Dominique Chasse, encouraged by Marmontel, dared to appear minus the stiffened short "panier" of the time. His costume was very much criticized by the public, especially in higher circles, who considered it "horribly indecent and degrading" for the French stage.

A few years before Mademoiselle Huberty's experiment, the famous dancer Vestris abolished the masks of some of the characters in the Ballet, and after him Noverre got rid of the tall wigs. A daring attempt to reform the traditional costume of the ballerina was made by Mademoiselle Sallé. Trying to introduce the tunics of Antiquity into the Ballet, she "dared to appear without paniers and with nothing on her head, and had only a corset and a short skirt of mousseline, which was draped in the style of a Greek statue." She met with such hostility from the administration and the "maîtres de ballet" of the Paris Opera that she had to leave the theatre. It was only later, in 1734 in London, when she appeared at Covent Garden, that she successfully realized her ideas in the ballets *Pygmalion* and *Ariadne*.

After the French Revolution, when the fashions of antiquity were introduced into ordinary life, the classical costume created by Talma gradually became a favourite on the stage. When in 1791 a singer, who had only a couple of bars to sing, appeared in *Œdipus at Thebes* in a woollen tunic with bare neck, arms, and legs, "the public very much admired his costume and applauded him loudly."

CHAPTER IX

THE NINETEENTH CENTURY

DURING the nineteenth century actors on the European stage were dressed with much less taste and æsthetic sense than in the preceding centuries, and their costumes in dramatic and especially in operatic shows frequently consisted of a mixture of different periods and ridiculous fancies. Until the last quarter of the nineteenth century nearly every production of what is known on the stage as a "costume play" was a sort of Bedlam as regards dresses. Actors and actresses not only wore modern dresses adapted to different periods, but used historical costumes of different styles in the same play, and these were far from being historically accurate.

In the nineteenth century more and more theatrical companies began to be managed by private individuals or run on the "commonwealth" system, and often there were no available means to make expensive or even new costumes for every play in their répertoires. Besides, in the nineteenth century the new idea was growing among actors and managers that the only thing which mattered on the stage was "acting," while environment and appearance were considered comparatively unimportant. As the result of such an outlook costume on the stage very often became almost a "quantité négligeable." Moreover, the not over-educated ladies and gentlemen of the acting profession, especially those employed by private management, were in most cases under the direction not of cultured artists, but of commercial "showmen," and had no proper artistic supervision. The theatrical traditions of the costume of the past were not particularly well understood by actors and actresses of the nineteenth century, and got sadly jumbled up with badly digested new ideas on "naturalism" and historical accuracy. The confusion resulting produced those so-called stagey or absurd operatic theatrical costumes, totally with-

135

out style, examples of which we still see quite often on the provincial operatic stage and even in the "spectacular productions" of certain famous managements. As a matter of fact, many modern cinema historical shows, with their nonsensical, ignorant, and grossly exaggerated costumes, completely lacking any creative imagination or understanding of period, may be justly considered as the successors to that traditional stage costume of the nineteenth century.

As usual, of course, the actors, and especially the actresses, paid much more attention to the question of how their personal physique might look its best on the stage than to solving any artistic problem of style or historical truth in their costume. Tieck wrote in 1825: "Actresses take every opportunity to change their dress during the performance. The men imitate them and are almost more coquettish than the women." The poet Heinrich Heine, writing on the French stage in 1837, said: "The kept women (femmes entretenues) display a terrible passion to exhibit themselves on the stage—a passion in which vanity and calculation are united—because on the stage they can display their bodies to the best advantage, be noticed by aristocratic debauchees and also admired by the greater public. These ladies, whom one sees particularly in the smaller theatres, do not usually get any salary. On the contrary, they pay the directors a certain sum monthly for the favour of being allowed to show themselves on the stage. As a result one very seldom knows where the actress begins and the courtesan ends, where the comedy stops and the call of nature begins, or where poetry becomes lewdness." The Director of the Viennese Stadttheater, Heinrich Laube, writing in the 'seventies said: "It is almost impossible to hire an actress, because as they spend fantastic sums on stupid toilettes, they ask for fantastic salaries. Velvets and silks are worn by all women, even by those who have no right to them. Even in scenes laid on country roads they are to be seen with endless trains, looking from head to foot like Queens of Hearts in playing cards."

It cannot be said that the dramatic and operatic actors of the seventeenth and eighteenth centuries were people of very liberal education or saintly morals, yet, as the theatre was not at that time such a widespread commercial public institution as it became in the nineteenth century, and the repertoires were more or less limited to one style of play and directed by people of a certain æsthetic sense and knowledge, they had the opportunity of getting that amount of artistic education sufficient to understand the plays they acted and the character of the costumes they wore. The difference between the influence of the theatrical directors of the seventeenth and eighteenth centuries on the mentality of actors and that of the "Tom, Dick, and Harry," helter-skelter, provincial managers of the nineteenth century, is more than obvious if one recalls the names of some of those directors. People like Shakespeare, Ben Jonson, Inigo Jones, Racine, Corneille, Molière, Lully, Dryden, Piranesi, the Bibienas, Gonzago, Marmontel, Voltaire, Diderot, Lessing, Gluck, Grétry, Garrick, Sheridan, Goldoni, Carlo Gozzi, and others then inspired the theatre. The *Commedia dell' Arte* shows were directed by people of taste and high culture, and its actors were people of understanding and masters of their art. Il Ruzzante or Angelo Beolco, a philosopher, poet, and actor, whom some call the "Italian Shakespeare," contributed greatly to the development and success of the *Commedia dell' Arte*. Francesco Andreini, the well-known actor, who played the part of the Capitano and then created the parts of the Sicilian Doctor, a variation of the Bolognese Doctor, and Falcirone the Magician, was also a writer and poet. He knew five languages, and could play all kinds of musical instruments. His wife Isabella Andreini was known, not only for her good looks and clever acting, but for her brilliant education. She gained the respect of Tasso, and was elected a member of several Academies. Nearly all the actors of the *Commedia dell' Arte,* besides being playwrights and poets (since they had to improvise), could sing and dance and do acrobatics and play some kind of musical instrument. "The *Lovers* study history, fables, rime, and prose, and the conceits of language. Those whose job it is to make folk laugh rack their brains to invent new farces, not from any wish to sin, or to make others sin, nor to praise vice and folly, but to earn an honest living by arousing laughter with their covert quips and bizarre inventions." The great interpreter of the part of Scaramouche, Tiberio Fiorilli, was an acrobat and musician of distinction.

The idea introduced into actors' heads in the "Sturm und Drang" period in Germany and later by the French Romantics, that they must "feel" before and above everything else, and that intelligence and technique were only of secondary importance, was almost unknown to theatrical folk before the nineteenth century. Furthermore, a certain amount of taste and theatrical sense cannot be denied to those Italian and German princes and Dukes, nor to Queen Elizabeth of England, Philip II of Spain, Louis XIV, Catherine II of Russia, and to other Mæcenas who, in their day, more or less occupied the position of the nineteenth-century manager. Although these people ran their theatres merely for their own amusement and not for the public, their actors had the chance to become sufficiently educated not to wear, for example, a Polish hat in the rôle of an ancient Greek (as was done by an actor in 1825), an eighteenth-century French coat with Spanish sixteenth-century trunk hose, white stockings and buckled shoes with imitation diamonds, and carry a rapier studded with paste diamonds. Before the nineteenth century people worked on the stage principally for the sake of art, very often sacrificing the necessities of life to their work for the joy and inner satisfaction which that work was giving them. But in the nineteenth century the theatre began to be merely a means of earning a livelihood, and the question not only arose of how above all else to please the increasingly powerful class of the bourgeoisie and to satisfy its limited outlook, but also of how to make more money by bringing personalities into prominence and by economizing and sacrificing the artistic side of the production, which gradually became the least important. The more greedy for personal gain and comfortable living the actors were, the lower the level of the acting and the productions sank, and the cheaper and the more absurd their costumes became.

During the whole of the nineteenth century, even after the establishment of the naturalistic "Meininger" theatre by Duke George II of Saxe-Meiningen in 1874, artistic ignorance, lack of understanding of the style of a costume in reference to that of the play and to the character, and absence of taste in the matter of costumes were often quite incredible. Even in the Berlin State theatre, which was under the direction of no less a person than the great producer, actor and playwright Iffland, the actresses in 1812, playing the parts of Mary Stuart, Lady Macbeth, and Portia, appeared dressed in odd compositions of Empire fashions with a mixture of historical details from various other periods. The unhappy Mary Stuart, for instance, was convulsed with grief in her prison in a black evening dress with high Empire waist and a décolleté cut too wide and too low, with fashionable curls, and a long transparent veil. In 1825 the famous Romantic actress, Mademoiselle Mars, of the Comédie Française, appeared as Eleonora in *Tasso* in a dress of her own day, to which were added a small sixteenth-century Spanish ruff and puffs on the shoulders. Five years later the same actress played Doña Sol in Victor Hugo's *Hernani* in an evening frock of 1830 with the addition of transparent wide sixteenth-century Italian sleeves and a large French eighteenth-century "Chinese" hat decorated with a long, ridiculous feather. When representing Greek or Roman women in the nineteenth century, the actresses usually wore modern corsets and high-heeled shoes, and in 1890 Cordelia and Ophelia appeared on the French stage with "peg-top" décolleté busts, wasp waists, and long skirts with trains, as if they were about to go to a ball at the Grand Opera.

When in the 'sixties the bell-like "crinoline" came into fashion in France, the ladies of the theatre wore it even under their historical costumes. Hortense Schneider, the famous interpreter of Offenbach's *Belle Hélène,* wore in the title part of this operette a large bell-like cage of steel hung on her hips under a Greek costume. Frau Johanna Jackman-Wagner wore a crinoline in the part of Ortrud in *Lohengrin.* When the well-known German singer, Christine Hebbel-Enghaus, appeared in Weimar as a "star-guest" in Wagner's *Nibelungen,* her passion for fashion caused an unfortunate accident. Being a smart woman she naturally wore a crinoline to sing the part of the primitive Germanic Krimhild. Not having rehearsed her last scene, on falling dead on the stage the crinoline stood up around her like a bell, uncovering her "dessous" up to the waist to the great amusement of the public.

The crinoline of 1860 was much lighter and simpler than the farthingale of the sixteenth or the "paniers" of the eighteenth centuries. It had twenty-four metallic horizontal circles in it, and though much wider than the farthingale, weighed only about half a pound. As during this time the aim of smart women was to look as large as possible below the waist, they augmented the volume of the crinoline by wearing from three to six underskirts in addition, of varying lengths, and decorated the skirts of their dresses with "volants," made either of the same material as the dress or of lace. In 1859 the Empress Eugénie wore at a ball a dress of white satin decorated with not less than one hundred and three tulle "volants." As a contemporary said, the torso of a woman in a dress of this time "peeped out of the mass of skirts like the stem of a lily out of a barrel." The waisted bodice of the day dress was usually fastened high round the neck and finished with a small linen or lace collar, but the neck of an evening dress at this time was cut very low, exposing the shoulders and bosom not too modestly. The décolleté was often decorated with a frill or rows of frills called "Berte" made of ribbons and sometimes ornamented with rows of jewels. The "Berte" added greatly to the "chic" of the toilette, and was often worth much more than the whole dress itself. The voluminous crinoline prevented the arms from hanging naturally, and obliged the wearer to maintain a "teapot handle" attitude which made the tight sleeves of the fashion of 1845 seem out of harmony with the billowing skirts. This resulted in the reintroduction of the eighteenth-century sleeve "à la pagode," which began narrow at the shoulder and widened into the form of a bell from the elbow. In 1860 these sleeves, like the crinoline, were supported with metal strips, and were also decorated with "volants."

Although the stage costume of actresses in the nineteenth century was reminiscent of contemporary fashionable walking or evening dress, the men, who were unable to wear or adapt their undecorative everyday attire for historical and fantastic plays, used modern military uniforms together with the historical fashions and traditional stage costumes of the preceding periods, adapting them, as far as their frequently limited appreciation of truth and beauty would allow, to the taste of the time. The question of personal attraction played the most imporant part in the choice of the design and colour of the costumes. Thus the English tragedian Matthews found it advantageous to play Richard III in a fantastic adaptation of the Hussar uniform of his own time, and Robert Coates appeared as Romeo in 1810 at the Haymarket Theatre in a fancy dress of sky blue and red, with coat of the former colour and tights of the latter. A distortion of the sixteenth-century Spanish costume was popular with the actors of the nineteenth century, as was also the German "Landsknecht" and the so-called "Shakespearean" costume (a concoction of the Elizabethan and of the Italian fifteenth- and sixteenth-century dress). "The Italian" costume, which consisted of tights, a doublet and a beret, often decorated with plumes, was also a great favourite, especially with Italian tenors, and was used indiscriminately in the parts of Romeo, of the Duke in *Rigoletto,* of Alfred in

La Traviata, and in *The Huguenots.* The eighteenth-century "habit habillé" profusely decorated with cheap gold, silver, or ordinary lace and galons, the Swiss "peasant" costume, the Scots and the "Italian bandit" were other favourites, the last-named being especially popular for villains. The French dress of the end of the seventeenth century, called the "Molièresque" costume, usually made in dull brownish shades, was worn in all the seventeenth-century plays, and with the appearance of Wagner's *Ring* his Germanic costumes became a stock routine on the operatic stage, and were used with little modification in all "primitive" or "savage" plays. Even at the end of the nineteenth century, after the "Meininger" had already shown their naturalistic historical productions, it was common in the provinces and even in the big towns to see rococo coats put over Molièresque waistcoats (from beneath which appeared trunk hose or a sixteenth-century Spanish doublet), with three-cornered hats and cavalry swords borrowed from officer friends of the actors. About twenty-five years ago theatrical costumiers still existed who called any dress belonging to the eighteenth century "the French costume," and who saw no difference in cut between the English Restoration, French Regency, Louis XV's and Louis XVI's periods. I myself once had the pleasure of working with a gentleman who was considered a "specialist" in the making of theatrical costume, and who boldly combined Elizabethan dress with that of the time of Henry VIII, calling such concoctions "Shakespearean costume." As for "the Italian costume," according to his understanding it included something from every dress designed by the artists of the whole Renaissance plus that of the operatic bandit "Sparafucile" and of the Neapolitan cigarette-box macaroni eater.

The costumes of small characters and supers were usually completely ignored by directors, and even in the Vienna Hofburg Theater at the beginning of the nineteenth century Austrian soldiers representing Mediæval people were allowed to appear on the stage in their long military gaiters. It was quite customary to see actors playing small historical parts on the stage in their street boots, and wearing a combination of odds and ends of costumes of different periods taken almost haphazard from the wardrobe, with their own collars and cuffs peeping out.

Among the most important reformers of theatrical costume in the first half of the nineteenth century, who, by the way, had very little influence in their time on the way actors were dressed, were the Germans—Iffland, Goethe, Count Brühl, and Tieck. The greatest German poet Goethe was the director of the Ducal theatre of Weimar, Brühl was the "Intendant" of the Court theatre in Berlin, and Tieck was the dramatist attached to the Court theatre at Dresden.

Goethe wrote to Eckerman: "The decoration of the stage in general should harmonize with the colours of the costume." He wanted to have the sets "more or less brownish in tone, in which the colours of the costumes could stand out freshly. If, however, this same favourable colour for the background cannot be used, and there is, for instance, a red or yellow room, a white awning, or a green garden, the actors should be very careful as regards their costume, and avoid wearing the colours of the stage-setting." As we see, Goethe's theory on theatrical costume aimed at harmonizing the costume with the background and at putting the actors' figures into plastic prominence on a soberly coloured background.

The realist Iffland, who introduced "Middle-class drama"—"das Bürgherliche Schauspiel"—to the German stage, tried to bring with it the realistic middle-class dresses of the period also. He was opposed, however, to copying the colours usually worn in the ordinary life of that time owing to their dullness. In 1807 he wrote, in his *Almanach für Theater und Theaterfreunde:* "Now that in everyday life there are only three colours for men's clothes, black, brown, and blue, and for women almost only white, it is not easy to tell the difference on the stage between a gentleman, a servant, lover or uncle, or between a lady and a soubrette. In the theatre there are performances in which all the men are in black and all the women in white."

Count Brühl was in favour of historical costume in historical plays, and fought against the stubbornness, obstinacy, and prejudices of his company. "On the Berlin stage," he wrote, "one can see costumes of different centuries on the stage at the same time." As regards women's costumes, he says that they were as near as possible to the contemporary fashions, and adds that "to give people a sight of a beautiful arm or bosom the actresses are ready to act a nun without sleeves and in a low-cut neck without a neck-kerchief." Brühl's experiments in reforming productions from an historical point of view gave rise to strong opposition on the part of numbers of actors and influential people, amongst whom was none less than Goethe and the famous actor Edward Devrient. On the 15th of October, 1817, Count Brühl produced his first play according to his ideas. It was the opera *Alceste* by Gluck, and the costumes and settings were designed by the architect and painter Schinkel, an authority on the Antique, and well known in theatrical history for improving the construction of the stage and auditorium. Two and a half years after the first production of *Alceste* Goethe wrote to Brühl praising his effort to present costumes on the stage in keeping with the environment, but saying at the same time that if the strict following of those principles which seek to assure characteristic originality to each new play and to each new part is hardly possible financially for a Royal theatre, it is utterly impossible for the others. He advised Brühl to use more "liberality" and freedom in his productions. Devrient complained, like hundreds of actors before him and thousands since, who were afraid that a good costume would attract more attention than they themselves, that Brühl was merely turning the actor into an interesting dressed-up doll. From pictures of Brühl's costumes, which he began to publish in 1819, one can see that, although these

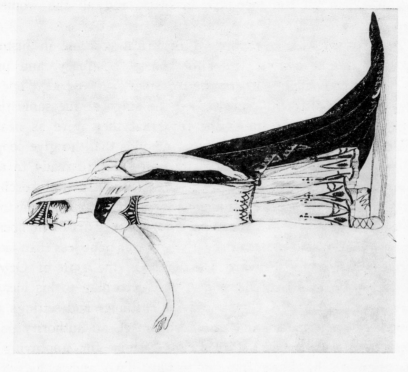

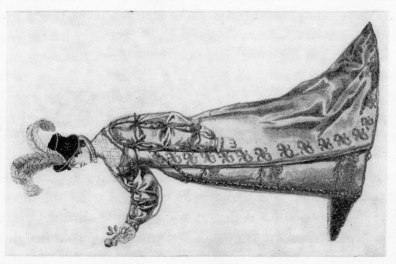

COSTUME OF THE PRINCESS OF EBOLI   OPERATIC COSTUME OF SEMIRAMIS

Brühl's production of 'Don Carlos'

by Schiller

Berlin   *About 1820*

were always harmonious in conception and decorative, they were still not always historically accurate nor strictly characteristic of the parts for which they were made. In his costumes for women he made the same mistakes as those of which he accused contemporary actresses. These dresses were a compromise between the "modes" of about 1820 and the fashions of the epochs of the plays he produced.

Tieck, whose ideas on stage production and costume were very similar to those expressed by the symbolists and "stylisateurs" of the end of the nineteenth and beginning of the twentieth centuries, also criticized Brühl, and in 1825 wrote: "Is the stage a mirror of the time by which we are to learn something about different costumes? Each art has only its own particular original truth, and does not know the *real truth,* which only exists outside its domain. Art lives and moves in its own element only." Tieck quite rightly says that costume should depend only upon the manner and style in which the play is written, and should be "as the poet saw it in his imagination." As regards French costume in the seventeenth and eighteenth centuries, which was historically inaccurate but true to the meaning and style of pseudo-classic French tragedy, he says that "in the poetry, moods, and passions of those tragedies there was the same unnatural quality as there was in the costume with which, however, they harmonized." In one of his criticisms of an historical play, Tieck wrote that mere naturalism on the stage is repulsive, and that naturalism is opposed to the true aim of the Drama. "We steal in a clumsy and almost pedagogical manner," said he, "from churches, graveyards, chronicles, books of heraldry, and museums in order faithfully to portray a buckle or an ugly head-dress, as if our spectators were mediæval tailors for whom all this accuracy was perhaps of the highest importance. And there are to-day a good many *actors* who have quite fallen in love with all these futilities!" Tieck's own idea on the subject of costume on the stage was seen in his production of *A Midsummer Night's Dream* in Berlin in 1840. The Athenians appeared in the costume of Shakespeare's day, and the workmen as artisans of the period of the production. He thought the *style* of Shakespeare's poetry could be best expressed by means of the costume worn in Shakespeare's time, but that the popular *Commedia dell' Arte* spirit of the clown scenes could be conveyed to his spectators most satisfactorily by means of the more familiar contemporary costume.

Goethe's picturesque theories and Brühl's ideas had, however, very little influence on dress on the contemporary stage, and Tieck's even less. The rococo tragedy of Schiller, for instance, *Kabale und Liebe,* was played in Berlin in the middle of the nineteenth century in modern dress, and the Bohemian prince, in Weber's opera *Der Freischutz,* appeared on the stage of the Grand Opera in Paris in 1841 in a kind of Turkish dress, and his numerous suite wore besides Bohemian, fantastic Turkish and even Chinese costumes.

Towards the middle of the nineteenth century, to create artistically harmonious productions, serious artists began sometimes to be employed by continental theatrical directors to design costumes and scenery. In Paris Delacroix, Delaroche, Gustave Doré, Détaille, and others worked for the stage. In Germany Kretschmar, Louis Corinth, Stuck, and Bocklin designed the scenery (the latter for Wagner's *Ring*).

A very strong movement on behalf of naturalism and historical truth on the nineteenth-century stage, which influenced the theatre throughout the world, was due to the Duke of Saxe-Meiningen, who opened, with his producer Kronegg in 1874, his naturalistic theatre at Meiningen. Their aim was to give an exact copy of real life and to make history live again on the stage. As the duke was wealthy his experiment was very thorough, and it all seemed very convincing to the majority of theatrical folk and others. A great many people had the chance of seeing the Meininger troupe, as it toured widely with its costumes, sets, furniture, and props. Every

historical costume in this company was absolutely correct, even over-
loaded with details and characteristic touches of the period. But the
costumes of the Meininger failed to express the spirit of the plays,
and lacked the artistic truth of which Tieck had spoken fifty years
before. The naturalistic details of the Meininger costumes distracted
the spectators, and their lifelikeness made them merely dull and un-
expressive from the auditorium. The actors seemed more like mannequins in an historical museum or waxwork show, and the productions have been compared with animated but emotionally unconvinc-
ing historical or domestic pictures. Even the rich and powerful Duke
George II of Saxe-Meiningen could not carry this naturalism to
perfection. It was beyond even his power to persuade his actresses
to take off their modern corsets while wearing historical costume.
Still, as naturalness on the stage, even when quite absurd, has always
been very popular with people who suffer from lack of imagination,
as is the case with the majority, the Meininger had many followers
among theatrical folk, and even more among the public.

Until the beginning of the twentieth century the Western theatre
was under the spell of naturalism. In England the Meininger found
imitators among actors and producers, and above all in Sir Herbert
Tree. In France there was Antoine, in Germany Brahm, in the United
States David Belasco, in Russia the Imperial Dramatic theatres, and
later the Moscow Art theatre, which brought scenic naturalism, as it
seemed at the time, to the greatest pitch of perfection.

In its first productions the Moscow Art theatre, headed by Stanis-
lavsky and Nemirovitch-Dantchenko, slavishly followed the traditions of the Meininger, transplanting them on to Russian soil. On the
opening night, in the production of a poetical and historical Russian
play, *Tzar Fyodor Ivanovitch,* the costumes of the Tzar, of the boyards,
and of the Moscow people were exact replicas of historical documents,
and made as far as possible of the genuine old materials. The long
bejewelled brocade coats of the boyards had fur collars and were lined

throughout with fur, which made them so heavy that it seemed almost impossible for the actors to breathe, let alone move in them. They wore fur hats of such height that the spectators must have been in constant fear of them toppling off the heads of the actors. In the revolt scene on the bridge over the river Yaousa the Moscow mob were as naturalistically dirty and shabby as the original mob must have been, but the costumes of the "Lovers," although correct historically, were much prettier and smarter than they could ever actually have been this is being due to the theatrical convention which was too strong for even naturalists such as those of the Moscow Art theatre to overcome. In the production of *Julius Cæsar* the stage was so filled with brass armour, helmets, weapons, ample togas, and various minute details of costume and properties, that Shakespeare's play was completely drowned. The heights of naturalism, however, were reached when the Moscow Art theatre presented Leo Tolstoy's *The Power of Darkness* and Gorki's *The Lower Depths,* which latter production was afterwards copied by Max Reinhardt in Berlin, at his little Unter den Linden theatre, formerly "Schall und Rauch" cabaret, at the time when this producing director was still a follower of Brahm and a naturalist. The clothes of the lodgers in Gorki's play, produced by the Moscow Art theatre, were so torn and dirty that if it had not been for the exaggerated make-up of the actors, which was in great favour on the Continental stage at that time, the illusion that one was actually amongst tramps in a lodging-house would have been complete. But this "natural" dirtiness and shabbiness detracted from the social and romantic spirit of Gorki's play, making it lose its significance on a grand scale, and reducing it to a casual affair, a kind of illustration to a newspaper article.

The reaction against naturalism in costume and production in Russia at the end of the nineteenth century was started by a rich business man, Savva Mamontov, who ran an operatic theatre in Moscow called "The Private Opera." He engaged artists to design the settings and costumes for his theatre, who assisted this new movement by ignoring "reproduction" and historical accuracy, seeking only artistic composition of forms and colours in their work. They attempted, through the medium of painting and design, to give their own impressions and individual understanding of the operas, for which they devised the costumes and settings. They aimed at creating an harmonious ensemble on the stage of the lines, forms, and colours of the décor and costumes, and when they found it necessary for their purpose they sacrificed not only historical truth but nature also. Costume, in the hands of these painters, who were influenced more by the works of art and poetry of the past than by history or the actual conditions of life, became a work of pictorial art, and not the mere reproduction of history or actuality which it had been in the Meininger or later in the Moscow Art theatre. In order to achieve tonal harmony with the décor the artists employed by Mamontov frequently had complete costumes made of hand-painted designs, and furs and armour were often painted on cloth and canvas as substitutes for the real materials. Many of these costumes were made of specially dyed silks, velvets, etc. The stage work of most of these painters was inspired by the primitive Russian paintings, the Antique ikons and frescoes, and by the popular coloured prints and other decorative works of ancient peasant art. No doubt the French impressionist and symbolist painters, and those of the early Italian Renaissance also, influenced these Russian artists to a great extent, and their comic costumes, revealing their love for the grotesque, were often inspired by the dresses of the funny characters of the *Commedia dell' Arte*. Among the Russian reformers of theatrical costume who began their work for the stage at the end of the nineteenth century, one must mention the artists Vroubel, Konstantin Korovin, Nicholas Sapounov, and Serge Soudeikin. The first two created that highly picturesque "fairy-tale" stylized pseudo-Russian costume which later the whole of Europe and America witnessed in the performances of Diaghileff's

Russian Ballet and the Russian Opera, and which has now become traditional and almost commonplace. Sapounov and Soudeikin derived inspiration from the Mediæval and Early Renaissance tapestries, from old Russian china figures, Russian peasant woodcuts and toys, and from the seventeenth and eighteenth century Italian and French theatres. The former (who died in 1912) always seemed to me more Western in his art than the latter. In spite of all the Russian spirit in his paintings, the French influence of Gauguin, Manet and Renoir, and even of Watteau, is felt in them. Some of his "natures mortes" could be placed on the same wall with the works of the best French masters. The crudely and brightly coloured grotesque and comic inventions of Soudeikine, showing the influence of the primitive decorative Russian peasant art and of old Russian China, are known in Europe through the "Chauve Souris" theatre run by Nikita Balieff.

In western Europe the evolution of theatrical costume in the nineteenth century was furthered by those who advocated the "symbolic" drama, and such playwrights as Oscar Wilde and Maeterlinck had an undeniable influence on the stage costume of their time. The former, when planning his production of *Salome,* thought it was essential that the colours worn by the actors should convey the symbolic meaning of the characters. He did not wish the actors to sink into the décor, nor to stand away from it as separate entities, but tried to create a significant scheme of symbolical colourings. Thus, he wanted to see Salome herself in black and green against a blue and gold background, Herod in gold, the Romans in purple, the Jews in yellow, and so forth. Maeterlinck's influence on costume was not perhaps as direct as Wilde's, and arose through his little dramas, concerned mainly with "the life of the soul," and not with outer events and happenings in human existence. To suit these dramas of Maeterlinck efforts were made (among others by the French producer Lugné Poe) to devise costumes based on reality, but at the same time suggestive of something not of mortality. It was essential, therefore, that neither the cut nor colour of these costumes should be obtrusive, and when dealing with historical periods, characteristic ornamentation was disposed of, and the dresses were kept as simple as possible, and the colour scheme subdued and even monotonous. Thus a kind of "abstract" costume for the stage was created belonging to no definite period or place, and depending largely upon lighting for colour and plastic effect. The forms of this costume were largely inspired by the Italian Primitives, by the Greek draperies, by old Germanic dresses, and by the paintings of Puvis de Chavannes.

CHAPTER X

THE TWENTIETH CENTURY

AT the beginning of this century the Meininger naturalism was still in full bloom in the majority of theatres, but those known on the Continent as "advanced" and experimental were making a firm stand against the mere reproduction of photographs of nature and historical documents. The leaders of the protest, as at the end of the nineteenth century, were the modern playwrights, a few producing directors, and those "modernist" artists who had ousted the old professional scenery designers and costumiers from the pioneer theatres.

Without doubt the Ballet performances of Diaghileff, known outside Russia as the "Russian Ballet," in which painters of great talent, who followed the traditions of the Mamontov Opera, played such a prominent part, gave the strongest blow to the old professional theatrical "décorateurs" and costumiers in western Europe.

At the time of Diaghileff's début in France, the main object of settings in the conservative and popular theatres was to establish an *illusion* of reality on the stage, deceiving the eyes of the spectators by means of canvas, cardboard, and painting. Half-tones and pale colours—greys, sky-blues, washy pinks, and dirty mauves were all in favour. The interior settings in dramatic theatres were usually made naturalistically as three-walled rooms with ceilings, while the operatic or ballet décors, representing different interiors or exteriors, were painted in perspective on drop-arches, backings, and borders of canvas following the tradition of the seventeenth-century decorators. The costumes were designed quite independently from the décor, and therefore had nothing in common with it, but were usually as dull pictorially.

The conception of décor and costume of Diaghileff's artists was inconceivably different from that of those people whose profession it was to supply scenery and costumes to the theatres. The former, like other modernist artists who had come to work in the theatre before them, intensely disliked the perspective settings and what in French is called "trompe l'œil" effects. They were also against the imitation of nature, which led to constructing "real" houses and rooms full of details on the stage, in the manner of the Meininger. They were all for imagination, simplicity, and broadness of conception and execution in their sets and costumes. They were painter-poets, whose aim it was not to reproduce what each of us can see every day, but to transport the spectator into a world of pictorial fantasy. For this purpose they created bold designs, using brilliant colours. They were often satisfied with a single picturesque back-cloth and a couple of wings or side curtains for a show. For them the costumes, properties, and furniture were part of their pictorial composition, and blended with the back-cloths in a symphony of colours.

If other artists, who collaborated with Diaghileff later on, at the end of his activities, gave up the exclusively painted settings and used schematic "constructions" instead, they still remained imaginative artists. Yegor Jacoulov and Pavel Tchelistchev, in their constructions and material suggestions, instead of sets in Diaghileff's productions of *Pas d'Acier* and *Ode,* were even farther removed from the idea of representing nature on the stage than those artists who preferred painting on back-cloths.

The influence of Diaghileff's decorators, who were, by the way, sometimes given undue prominence in his ballets, and of other modernist artists, who used the stage for the purpose of unfolding their compositions, spread rapidly, and after the War they had made such a marked impression that there was a growing tendency in most of the eminent productions of dramatic shows, and especially in operas and ballets, to overstress the visual side of the "mise en scène," the actors, singers, and dancers, and even the producing directors, being at the mercy of the designers of the costumes and settings. It was this tendency which led to the misapplication of the word "production."

The essential part of the work of a producing director is to interpret a play by means of the acting of single actors and of the ensemble of actors, and not by the invention of scenic environment. He devises and uses such costumes and surroundings as will assist the acting and his interpretation of the play; but even now it is a common error to confuse the word "production" with the ensemble of costumes and décors devised either by the producing director himself or by a scenic artist who often has not even read the play. The latter, in creating his artistic compositions, usually without the close guidance of the producer, does not assist the production of a play, but rather tends to obscure and frustrate its meaning, reducing the stage to an exhibition of animated pictures assisted (from my point of view, hindered) by action, words, and music. However, work of this description is often greeted with eulogies in contemporary newspapers, and not a few talented actors and directors have been insufficiently appreciated on account of these obtrusive and dazzling creations of scenic designers. There have, on the other hand, been many producing directors who owe their fame to the happy choice of original scenic designers, and again there have been many scenic designers who have made their reputations thanks only to some producing directors, who have actually invented, planned, modelled, and lighted their settings, for which the scenic designers, whose only work has been the painting, have received full credit. Especially is this the case in France, since the production at the beginning of our century of Debussy's *Pelléas* at the Opéra Comique, when the scenery, painted by a well-known artist, Jusseaume, met with great approbation.

The influence all over Europe at the present time of the real painters who have contributed their services to the stage is enormous, and the curtain can scarcely go up on even a second-rate production of a revue or musical comedy without the names of Braque, Derain, Marie Laurencin, Leger, Picasso, Larionov, Gontcharova, Juan Gris, Othon Friez, R. Dufy, Utrillo, etc., occurring to one's mind, although those who actually designed the production may remain in ignorance of them. The characteristic poster-like designs of the late Lovat Fraser are adapted in cheap colour schemes in almost every production of a seventeenth or eighteenth century play on the London stage, and in many "fairy" productions one sees the influence of the book illustrations of Dulac, while many modern English musical shows recall the illustrations of the pre-war *Münchener Jugend* or of *Rezniczek*. Insipid, tasteless, and exaggerated imitations of settings and costumes designed by Bakst are now shown not only in every theatrical "spectacular" production, but also annoy one on the screen. Even the works of such painters as Manet, Renoir, Gauguin, Van Gogh, Cézanne, Henri Rousseau, and others who were never connected with the theatre are often used and reduced to commonplaces by the creators of spectacular enterprises.

The majority of the painters who left their easels to work in the theatre were attracted to it mainly because of the apparent possibility of being able to paint their pictures on a large scale. They frequently knew nothing of the stage, and were not particularly interested in the history of costume, often finding it sufficient to borrow indiscriminately from pictures in manuals, making alterations *ad libitum* to suit their own colour schemes. As examples of the ignorance of some painters in the matter of historical costume and even of their contempt for it, I can mention here two cases from my own personal experience as a producing director. When I dared to point out to one artist—quite well known—that in making the costumes for a French Louis XVI scene he had mixed the genuine fashions of this period with the genuine fashions of the Louis XV and even the Louis XIV periods, he replied that he had "created a fantasy." Actually he had simply copied a few of the Louis XVI, a few of the

Louis XV, and a few of the Louis XIV costumes from books with which I happened to be familiar, and coloured them to suit his own taste. Another artist, even more famous, supplied me with a design for the costume of the hero of Wagner's opera *Der Fliegende Holländer,* which represented a gentleman in a Restoration Court dress. When I remarked that this gentleman did not suit the character or the style of Wagner's opera, the artist, quite hurt, retorted: "I don't see why the chap could not dress like that."

When realizing their purely picturesque ideas on the stage, painters seldom stop to consider that the art of painting is static, whereas that of the stage is essentially dynamic and that that dynamic quality is expressed by the living and moving three-dimensional actor. The main object of most of them has always been to reproduce on a large scale the compositions of background and people devised in their small sketches or paintings. Costume was merely a detail of these compositions designed to blend with the decorative background and make the actor appear as part of the scenery, reducing him as far as possible to two dimensions. In order to complete the desired effect, in some advanced productions with picturesque settings and costumes the suffering actors were condemned to almost complete immobility on the stage. Some producing directors, who favoured the ideas of certain painters, attempted to invent a new type of acting, of restricted movements and artificial intonations, in keeping with the décor, but of course met with much protest on the part of the actors, who objected to being reduced to puppets. It occurred to certain theorists that this idea of two-dimensional puppets was just what was needed, and that it would be a good thing to oust the live actor from the theatre altogether. Others dallied with the idea of having the characters of a play painted on the background, with actors to speak and sing off stage. This fight between actors and the new theorists, however, did not last long, and was confined to a few experimental theatres, newspaper articles, and books.

The actors won, but the result was an unsatisfactory compromise, the painters continuing as far as possible to ignore both actor and producing director, devising their picturesque costumes and painted décors simply with a view to spectacular sensation and to give the public something to look at, while the actors continued to ignore the costume and scenery designers.

The "sculpturesque" and "stylized" costume, together with three-dimensional settings, both formal and simplified, appeared as a protest against these experiments to reduce the person of the actor to something two-dimensional. The Swiss artist, Adolphe Appia, who became known to some people at the very end of the nineteenth century, was one of the most important advocates of three-dimensional formal settings, and the German producing director Georg Fuchs was prominent amongst the theorists of the "stylized" costume.

The object of Appia's mono-coloured three-dimensional settings composed of screens, cubes, steps, and formal suggestions of things such as rocks, trees, etc., was to give value to the actor by bringing his *three-dimensional self* into *spacial* harmony with the scenic surroundings. He simplified and generalized the forms of nature and architecture when devising his settings, so that the attention of the spectator should not be distracted from the action of the play by superfluous realistic details. He was not at all interested in staging enlarged paintings or in giving faithful representations of reality, but was anxious, as far as the interpretation and the atmosphere of the play would allow, to create in his scenic environment only suggestions of reality. He compensated for the "lack of colour" in these by lighting, by means of which he also accentuated the movements and forms of the actors.

Appia designed very seldom in his sketches human figures, but from those few which could be seen on them and from his production experiment in collaboration with Jacques Dalcroze at Hellerau, one can conclude that he was an adept of those formalized in the manner of the Greek draperies and of the Italian Primitives, indiscriminately coloured sculpturesque costumes, which were introduced on to the stage before him by some of the producers of Maeterlinck's plays.

Appia had many followers and even plagiarists who, however, revealed themselves in their desire to give prominence to all those trappings which Appia had devised solely for the benefit of the three-dimensional actor and the play. To many of these disciples, actors with their living bodies and movements, which would not fit in with their sculptural and static settings, were merely a nuisance, and on working out Appia's principles in their own way they found themselves arriving at the same conclusions as certain theorists of the picturesque settings and costumes had done. Thus, in order to achieve complete harmony between the décor and the characters in it, they found it necessary to substitute perfected "super" marionettes for actors, but this time of a three-dimensional kind.

The costumes designed by Gordon Craig, who drew inspiration for his décors from Appia, were either resembling the above-mentioned costumes of Maeterlinck's plays or were influenced by Beardsley or by the English pre-Raphaelites.

The theories and principles of Georg Fuchs, of which he wrote in 1899, and which were demonstrated at his theatre in Munich in 1907, were mainly based on the work of certain designers of the Munich school, such as Erler, Dietz and Th. Th. Heine, who had created "stylized" period dresses in drawings, and on the ideas of Goethe and Tieck.

From the point of view of Fuchs and his school naturalistic and historical costume was not sufficiently expressive for the interpretation of plays. He found further that pictorial costume, treated as a detail of the painted decorative background, was inadequate for a living actor, treating him as a piece of flat painting, and that the scupturesque costume with its limited colours was not sufficiently decorative. The "stylizators" reasoned that, as the attention of the spectators should be directed on the moving actors, it was essential that the pictorial costumes should be designed so as to help the movements and to stand out from the scenery. Again, inasmuch as the style and colours worn during one particular year of fashion are not usually expressive of the ideas and moods contained in a play, so the reproduction of fashion-plates on the stage would not satisfy the requirements of any production. They maintained that, as the ideas contained in a play represent the synthesis of a whole period of human thought, so the costume worn should consist of a synthesis of all those years of fashion which make up the ideology of the play. In other words, there should be no exact historical dating on the stage, but a creative synthesis, called stylization.

The "stylizators" would not, for instance, consider it necessary to dress *The Marriage of Figaro* of Beaumarchais in the French or Spanish dresses of 1784, because the ideology of the play embraces the whole of the eighteenth century, and because, although the action of the play is laid by Beaumarchais in Spain and the characters have Spanish names, the meaning of the play is essentially French. They would dress the play in costumes devised to form a synthesis of the French and Spanish fashions of the whole of the eighteenth century. If, instead of the comedy by Beaumarchais, they produced Mozart's opera on the same story, it would again be dressed differently, because the music is not characteristic of Spain, but of Vienna and Italy, etc. In this case the costume should consist of some of the elements found in Beaumarchais' comedy, but with certain additions of Italian character and with something giving the Court atmosphere of Vienna of Maria Theresa's time, and possibly also of homely Salzburg.

In opposition to the partisans of the sculpturesque costume, who did not care for colour apart from that supplied by lighting effects, the "stylizators" adhered to the picturesque in costume, although, like the former, they were against painted scenery and favoured three-dimensional settings built and coloured in such a way as to put the costumes of actors into prominence.

Stylized and exaggerated modern costumes are used at the present time for their super-realistic productions ("mises en scène surréalistes") by the partisans of "constructions" on the stage, the Russian producer Meyerhold and the German producer Piscator, for instance.

Bakst and Picasso must undoubtedly be placed foremost amongst artists who have designed stylized period costumes for the stage without theorizing about them. Both of these painters show a fine sense of movement, creating designs for living bodies in action and not static puppets. The former, in his Greek and Eastern costumes, presented an individual synthetic interpretation of the dresses of Antique Greece and of the Orient. His work for Diaghileff's "Cleopatra" and "Scheherazade" is still remembered by everyone who went to the Russian Ballet. The stylized Spanish costumes designed by Picasso for Diaghileff's production of De Falla's ballet, *The Three-cornered Hat,* although fantastic, created a genuine Spanish atmosphere, and were a relief after the romantic "costume espagnol" or the pseudo-naturalistic, cigar-box Spanish dress, which had become traditional on the stage since the appearance of Bizet's opera *Carmen,* and which is so much admired by the English Musical-Comedy patrons and by the American film producers. The symbolic cubistic costumes invented by Picasso for the characters of the French and American managers in Satie's *Parade,* the latter suggesting a skyscraper constructed as a human silhouette, were most expressive for the "surréalisme" of the piece.

The aim of the cubist-painters in designing their costumes as well as settings was not merely to give a reproduction of an object, but to extract from it, by means of the free composition of its elements, everything it could give in the way of æsthetic emotions. Picasso went even farther in his work than the other cubists. The French writer Guillaume Apollinaire, who was "le grand animateur" of the epoch of the cubists, says that in *Parade* Picasso *translates* the

GREEK COSTUMES
Bakst

ORIENTAL BALLET COSTUME
Bakst

reality. "Le motif n'est plus reproduit mais seulement représenté; il voudrait être suggéré par une sorte d'analyse synthèse embrassant tous ses éléments visibles et quelque chose de plus, si possible, une schématisation intégrale qui chercherait à concilier les contradictions en renonçant parfois délibérément à rendre l'aspect immediat de l'objet."

Besides cubistic, another type of costume appeared known as "expressionistic," based on the art theories of the Futurists, Expressionists, and certain Dadaists (who in point of fact all have very much in common), and which is sometimes similar to the cubistic costume.

The first efforts of expressionistic painting were made in Germany and Austria by the artist Kokoschka, who, in his portraits exhibited in Vienna in 1908, "was expressing the inner life of people," and by the group of North German painters, which was called "Die Brücke."

According to the ideas of expressionists, an artist does not give individually treated reproductions or his own impressions of people and nature in his works, but creates either compositions of people, landscapes, and objects, correcting, altering, or distorting them as his mind and vision desire, or, completely ignoring the forms of nature, builds absolutely freely compositions of shapes, lines, and colours.

Thus there are two types of expressionistic producing directors and scenic artists. The first, who follow the principles of Kokoschka, may be called expressionist-realists, and the latter, the more advanced ones, pure expressionists. Neither of these desires to represent stage characters and their environment in true life-like forms.

The first compose costumes and masks (or make-ups) of such elements and suggestions of reality as will most fully express the substance of the "dramatis personæ" of the play, and assist their movements and the rhythm of their action.

Amongst the earlier efforts of introducing "realistic-expressionism" on to the stage could be mentioned, for instance, the production of the director Jessner in Berlin, Meyerhold's production of Andreyev's *The Life of Man* in 1907, for which I devised the expressionistic settings and costumes, and my own Moscow production in collaboration with the artist George Annenkov of *A Bad Joke* by Dostoyevsky (1915).

The pure expressionists, who are opposed to the theatre of literature, and who object to movement on the stage prompted merely by logic ("das Logisch-Gedankliche," as the German Dadaists say), propound theories of action and tempo bearing no relation to anything but the *pure desire for movement*. They assert that the most expressive movements on the stage are the "mechanically eccentric" ones. Completely ignoring nature they seek to clothe the actor in such geometric or mechanical compositions of lines and shapes as will produce movements seemingly impossible for a normal human being, and of such a nature that "the spectator might well be surprised and even terrified at the possibilities of the human organism."

The German advocates of the purely expressionistic costume reason somehow as follows: the man is enclosed in the cubic, abstract space of the stage. Either the stage, taking the natural man into consideration, must be arranged according to the illusion of reality in such a way as to fit the natural man, or the natural man must be transformed to match the cubistic and abstract space of the stage. As the creation of the illusion of reality is not the aim of art, the transformation of the human body becomes necessary on the stage. Such transformation is made possible by costume and the mask. The lines of the costume which transform the natural man into a stage-man are devised to suit and to accentuate those movements which are necessary during the performance. There are four such transformations of the human figure (see the drawings on the next page); the first produces the effect of moving architecture; the second of a doll on hinges; the third of a mechanical organism, and the fourth of complete de-

MECHANICAL COSTUMES
Oscar Schlemmer

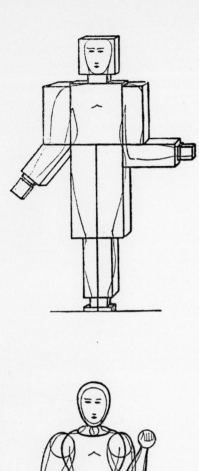
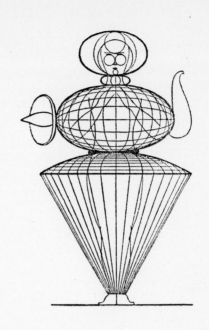
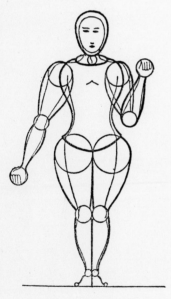
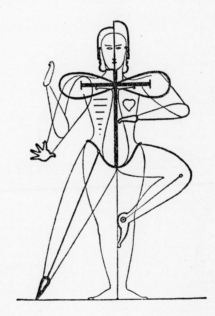

materialization. In the first transformation the cubic forms surrounding the human figure on the stage are transplanted on to the figure itself: the head, shoulders, chest, back, arms, and lower part of the body are covered with cubes. In the second transformation the forms of the body are made formal again by means of a stiff costume and a mask: the head becomes egg shape, the torso like a vase, etc. In the third the forms of rotation and direction are used. In the last transformation the actual costume is made in such a way as to be invisible, but the lines and shapes which symbolize the limbs, as seen in the drawing on the next page, are applied on top of the dress.

Yet despite these various and advanced experiments in the matter of costume and décor, the theatre of to-day, generally speaking, is still at least fifty years behind the times. Mechanism in all its manifestations has made extraordinary strides. The art of painting has undergone a complete metamorphosis, modern architecture has thrown the rules of old Vignola and Palladio to the winds, jazz and dissonance have superseded the orderly rhythms of the tuneful classic music, and to the lay mind the major poetry of to-day relies almost exclusively on combinations of onomatopoetic effects and novel rhythms with little "logical" or emotional content. The actual mechanics of the theatre, the equipment of the stage, lighting, etc., have advanced considerably too, and it seems strange that the *true* modern mentality has had so little effect on the purpose and the actual results of the modern theatre. But if one remembers that the theatre, unless financially supported as an institution of progressive culture, cannot exist without the attendance of people who seek nothing but easily digested entertainment on the stage, the reasons are not difficult to find.

The great masses of the public go to the theatre nowadays mainly to be stirred emotionally, and the majority to be stirred by trivial associations. It is only to those few who go to the theatre to enjoy the *art* of the theatre and its endless inventive possibilities, who are

HARLEQUIN

Picasso

GIRL WITH HOOPS

Picasso

stirred by *ideas,* and who are interested also in the life which lies beyond the daily routine, that a production which is modern in its form (and therefore in its content too) would be at all pleasing. In order to find any real interest on the stage, the greater public must have before them objects and people similar to those they meet with in their ordinary existence. Any "fantasy" and taste for beauty they may possess does not really react to much beyond saccharine platitudes, the style of coloured postcards, hairdresser types, or modern "hire-purchase" sets of furniture.

In the majority of "civilized" countries men go to the theatre nowadays mostly to be amused and to divert their minds from their everyday occupation of "making money." They do not wish to think while sitting in the stalls, nor to be troubled with the "unpleasant" truths of life, or by ideas of future possibilities of the world's progress, which threaten their money-making schemes. One of the greatest attractions for them in the theatre is the sex-appeal element of the productions, presented, of course, in the guise of "sweet" peroxided blondes with unquestionably virginal faces, but in the most ingenious, disturbing, and quite unexpected déshabillés. Of course, the richness of these scanty garments, and probably of their environment, symbolizing for them the everlasting financial prosperity of the world, also plays no small part in attracting men (and women also). The costumes of modern revues and musical comedies, like the plays themselves, satisfy the hypocrisy, the lightness of mind, the sexual instincts, and the taste for luxury of the present bourgeois generations. Of the same kind, if not still more extravagant, are the costumes in the spectacular "talkies," which in most cases do not represent anything else but animated and discordant mechanical reproductions of musical comedies. Not satisfied any more with the usual décolletés and retroussés, the designers of costumes for the shows of "lighter" nature denude the most unexpected parts of the actresses. I saw recently in a "talkie" a girl who was completely covered from head to foot, save for a generous display of thigh, and not long ago in a French revue some of the "figurantes" appeared showing their posteriors uncovered.

It was at the very end of the nineteenth century that women appeared with their torso bare or quite naked in a public show. Nowadays nakedness of both sexes in all kinds of entertainments, including those of the night-restaurants, is quite a commonplace "costume" all over the world. In less moral countries women often appear as naked as their mothers bore them, in the more moral ones with only a brassière and a "cache-sex."

Women, who are the great patrons of the more serious theatre to-day, go to the dramatic shows identifying themselves with the heroines on the stage, thus experiencing that stimulation of the emotions which Aristotle maintained to be the main purpose of the theatre. How often have young girls, sitting in the gallery of a theatre during a dramatic scene, been heard to exclaim, "That is exactly what I would have done!" So in the matter of costume women desire to identify themselves, and a dramatic play is doubly attractive for them if there are women in it wearing "the latest creations." The theatre has become such a social institution, in the most superficial sense of the word, that women go there enjoying the double pleasure of an entertainment, of a party, and of a mannequin parade, the actresses, especially in London, Paris, and New York, being looked to for the latest fashion.

Pandering to the taste of the public, the ladies as well as the gentlemen of the stage usually quite forget that even when acting in so-called "drawing-room" comedies and dramas, their costumes, although modern, must still be expressive of the characters they represent. Men acting in these plays appear dressed by expensive tailors, wearing lounge, morning, and evening suits, bowlers and top-hats, looking as if they had come from a shop window but a moment before, and expressing about as much as a puppet in the said window.

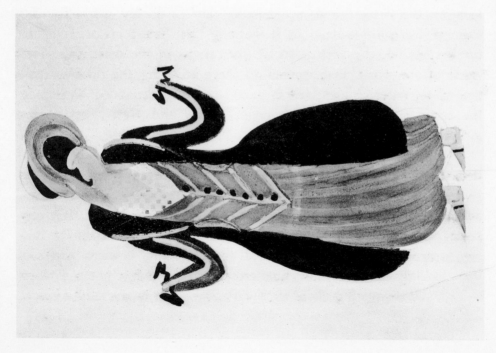

ORIENTAL COSTUMES
For an 18th century Comic Opera
Komisarjevsky

Actresses appear in modern plays parading about the stage as if they were in the salons of a "maison de couture," exhibiting the newest models and the more admired portions of their own complacent selves.

This combination by modern actresses of the rôles of both mannequin and interpreter of a part accounts to a great extent for the deterioration of their acting powers. It is quite impossible to act a part in a costume which exists independently merely as a dressmaker's creation, and is not "born" out of the understanding of the part and felt by the actor as the necessary form for the "skin" of the character. Unless this is felt, an actress is bound to be conscious of her dress apart from the character she is playing, trying to adapt her body and to move, not as the part, but as the dress requires. It is fatal for actresses to play frequently under such conditions and adapt themselves to dresses. As a consequence they lose the power essential for the stage, of visualizing themselves as they actually are, sometimes even ceasing to wish to be themselves, imagining that the dressmaker's garments on their bodies, the make-up on their faces, and the dyed hair on their heads make them more attractive. Dresses, and the flattery of dressmakers who make their money by understanding the psychology of women, act on most of them like soporifics and drugs, and all their behaviour begins to be directed by the things put on themselves. Women nowadays *act* in life to make their movements, manners, and even the words they utter match the garments they wear, and so on the stage, where they again appear enslaved by similar dresses, they cease to be able to, in fact do not wish to, act anything but the part they play in life.

"Smart" dresses had not always the influence on actresses that they have at the present time. Until the second half of the nineteenth century actors did not by any means belong to respectable society, and had no social standing whatever. Although "stylized" dresses modelled on the contemporary clothes worn by aristocratic and wealthy people were always used on the stage to suit the purposes of a show, these dresses were not the type worn by the actors in their private lives, but were merely used as a transformation for the stage. Again, the dresses worn by the women of the *Commedia dell' Arte* on the stage were quite unlike the everyday dresses of these poor strolling folk. The mannequin business of actresses started only in the eighteenth century, when the actual "robes de ville" began to be used for the stage. The movement for historical truth in the theatre, however, then the desire for romanticism, and later the naturalism of the Meininger, with its characteristic life-like and period dresses, succeeded to a large extent in suppressing the mannequin tendencies on the serious stage. In the shows of a lighter nature the exhibition of dresses continued, and by the end of the nineteenth century even the dramatic shows were influenced by this unsuitable flaunting of them.

From the artistic point of view the choice of a definite kind of costume for the production of a play depends on how the producing director intends to *interpret* the play on the stage. This interpretation of a play by means of "staging" ("mise-en-scène," or in German "Regie," or in Russian "putting the play up") depends on the individual understanding of the play and of the author by the producing director and, of course, on his general artistic and social outlook, i.e. on his philosophy of the theatre and of life. Therefore the first requirement of any stage costume should be the expression of this understanding and outlook, and its purpose should be to make the imagination of the spectators work in the desired direction.

The ignorance and disregard of the modern producers, while devising their costumes and sets, for the intentions and style of the dramatists are often unbelievable. Everyone who can *read* must be able to understand that Oscar Wilde's *Salome* was written as an ultra-modern fantasy. Beardsley quite rightly interpreted it by his *modern* illustrations. On our stage, however, the operatic producers, staging

Strauss' musical drama, make out of Wilde's play an historical show, and in its recent London production this play was treated, as far as costumes were concerned, as an Elephant and Castle melodrama, with Roman warriors clattering about in their hired armour like a collection of animated brass Russian samovars.

The naturalistic and genuine historical costume, since it is never expressive of the manner in which any artistic play is written or of the individual understanding of a play by any producer-artist, is quite senseless on the stage. Life is Life and Art is Art, and, as Tieck said, each of them holds its own truth. A magnificent dress taken direct from a museum on to the stage means nothing, and merely belongs to the category of "technical assistants." An actor dressed in a genuine historical costume on the stage cannot look anything other than a museum piece or a waxwork from Madame Tussaud's.

The second requirement of any stage costume is to assist the actor in his interpretation of the part and accentuate the expressiveness of his movements to reflect the rhythm of his creative mind. The costume should be designed with a view to the action of the wearer, varying its forms with him, and even changing its colours by means of stage lighting during the show. It is a well-known fact that certain plastic forms and certain combinations of colours produce definite effects on the human mind. Therefore the shape of costumes and the colour scheme of the ensemble of costumes as well as of each separate costume should not depend solely on the characteristics of the dramatis personæ or on decorative, pictorial, or sculpturesque ideas, but principally on those expressionistic effects and impressions which the producer wishes to create by the action of the play as a whole and of each separate moment of that action.

The third requirement of any stage costume is to place the actor into necessary prominence, and to make him in plastic and tonal harmony with his scenic environment, without ever being absorbed by it. Recently I saw a production in which the costumes and settings were designed by a well-known artist, and in which there was a scene where an old woman was strangled at night. The artist in question had provided a *white* dress for the actress and *white* cushions for the chair in which she sat. As a result her movements were scarcely visible to the audience, and half the drama of the situation was lost.

A producing director staging a *realistic* play should consider the fact that life-realism transferred into the realm of art becomes a form of expressionistic realism. Therefore the settings and costumes of a realistic play should be merely the most suitable forms in which to convey the inner meaning of the reality of the play to the public. Realistic stage costumes should, by their shape and colour, only suggest to the spectator a certain period and also the "milieu" in which the action of the play develops. They should be expressive and characteristic of the inner movement of the action of the play, of the characters wearing them, and of the idea of the interpretation of the play. Even in a realistic production every modern or historical dress should be transformed by the conception of the producing director into an expressive stage costume serving the purposes of the acting and production without destroying the required realism of the play.

The forms and colours of unrealistic stage costumes (symbolic or expressionistic) should be based on the imagination of the producing director, guided by his understanding of the art of the theatre, and by his conception of the play, of its style, and of its rhythm.

From my point of view, in a theatre in which actors are supposed to matter, it is infinitely preferable to act a play in some more or less commonplace dress which the audience can accept as a conventionality to be disregarded, than in the most magnificent pictorial, statuesque, or expressionistic costumes which have been devised by an artist independent of the idea of the production, and which neither express the meaning of the play nor correspond to the emotions and move-

ments of the actors, but merely reduce the theatre to pictorial, sculpturesque "panoramas" or wound-up mechanical circuses. How often
have I seen the performance of an actor ruined the moment he has
put on his costume. If in modern "costume plays" more attention
were paid to the fact that the costume should convey something to
the audience as part of the production, and stimulate the imagination
of the spectators, fewer plays of this type would be failures.

The costume plays a much bigger rôle on the stage than most
people realize. The actor should be a work of dynamic and rhyth-
mical theatrical art, and his costume is an essential part of that work
of art. The costume has as important a function on the stage as the
actor's face in order to produce the desired expression. The costume,
by its line, shape, and colours, is either an aid to an actor's movements or paralyses them. Costume either accentuates the transmission
of the actor's emotions to the audience or neutralizes or even destroys
them. The costume suggests to the audience the ideas which guided
the actor in his interpretation of the part. Even the best actor in a
costume which does not fulfil these requirements is like a statue by
a good sculptor on which some passer-by has put his overcoat, leaving
the head alone uncovered, from which the onlooker has to form his
opinion of the work.

INDEX